Maths
made easy

Key Stage 2
ages 10-11
Beginner

Author John Kennedy
Consultant Sean McArdle

Certificate

Congratulations to ....
(write your name here)
for successfully finishing this book.

 You're a star!

 Penguin Random House

Decimal addition

Write the answer to each sum.

$$296.48 + 131.74 = 428.22$$
$$\text{1 1 1}$$

$$173.05 + 269.23 = 442.28$$
$$\text{1 1}$$

Write the answer to each sum.

$$491.83 + 137.84 = 629.67 ✓$$

$$964.71 + 321.26 = 1285.97 ✓$$

$$302.04 + 204.99 = 507.03 ✓$$

$$306.25 + 844.24 = 1150.49 ✓$$

$$471.93 + 755.26 = 1227.19 ✓$$

$$842.01 + 711.84 = 1553.85 ✓$$

$$675.82 + 105.23 = 781.05 ✗$$

$$137.82 + 399.71 = 537.53 ✓$$

$$465.24 + 605.27 = 1070.51 ✓$$

$$178.93 + 599.41 = 778.34 ✓$$

$$184.74 + 372.81 = 557.55 ✓$$

$$443.27 + 705.99 = 1149.26 ✓$$

$$563.23 + 413.98 = 977.21 ✓$$

$$703.95 + 685.11 = 1389.06 ✓$$

$$825.36 + 249.85 = 1075.21 ✓$$

$$529.33 + 482.56 = 1011.89 ✓$$

Write the answer to each sum.

$$421.79 + 136.25 =$$

$$192.31 + 241.73 =$$

$$558.32 + 137.94 =$$

$$501.84 + 361.93 =$$

$$227.66 + 142.07 =$$

$$275.31 + 239.33 =$$

$$153.31 + 189.02 =$$

$$491.44 + 105.37 =$$

$$253.71 + 562.41 =$$

$$829.25 + 163.74 =$$

Problems with negative numbers

What is the difference in temperature between Boston and Barcelona?

11°C

By how much would the temperature have
to go up in Boston to be the same as London?

9°C

City	Temperature
Boston	–9°C
Barcelona	2°C
London	0°C

City	Temperature
Athens	2°C
New York	–6°C
Tokyo	1°C

City	Temperature
Warsaw	–7°C
Zurich	–12°C
Rome	5°C

By how much is Athens warmer than Warsaw?

If the temperature went up by 5°C, what would it be in:

New York   – 1°C   Zurich   – 7°C   Warsaw   – 2°C

If the temperature went down by 6°C, what would it be in:

Tokyo   –5°C   Rome   – 1°C   Athens   – 4°C

The temperature outside is –11°C. If it rises by 7°C,
what is the new temperature?

–4°C

The temperature inside a shelter is 5°C.
The temperature outside is 12°C lower.
What is the temperature outside?

– 7°C

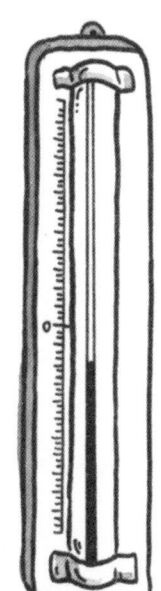

The frozen food compartments in a
supermarket are kept at a constant
temperature of –7°C. During a power cut
the temperature rises to 10°C.
By how much has the temperature risen?

17°C

The temperature at midnight is –8°C.
At midday it is 15°C higher.
What is the temperature at midday?

7°C

Square roots

What is the square root of 9?

3

If you do not know the square root of a number you can use the trial method.
What is the square root of 196?

I know the square root of 144 is 12, so it must be bigger than 12.
13 x 13 = 169 (too small)
15 x 15 = 225 (too big)
14 x 14 = 196
The square root of 196 is 14.

What is the square root of these numbers? Do your working out on paper if you need to.

16   144   36

4   64   49

81   121   100

Now try these.

324   256   400   289

What length are the sides of these squares?

Area = 361 cm^2

Area = 10 000 cm^2

            cm   cm

Comparing fractions

Which is bigger, $\frac{2}{3}$ or $\frac{3}{4}$? $\boxed{\frac{3}{4}}$

The common denominator of 3 and 4 is 12.

So $\frac{2}{3} = \frac{8}{12}$ and $\frac{3}{4} = \frac{9}{12}$

$\frac{3}{4}$ is bigger.

Which is bigger?

$\frac{1}{4}$ or $\frac{1}{3}$ ☐ $\frac{5}{6}$ or $\frac{7}{9}$ ☐ $\frac{1}{2}$ or $\frac{5}{8}$ ☐ $\frac{4}{9}$ or $\frac{1}{3}$ ☐

$\frac{2}{5}$ or $\frac{3}{8}$ ☐ $\frac{7}{10}$ or $\frac{8}{9}$ ☐ $\frac{8}{10}$ or $\frac{7}{8}$ ☐ $\frac{7}{12}$ or $\frac{2}{3}$ ☐

$\frac{2}{3}$ or $\frac{5}{8}$ ☐ $\frac{4}{15}$ or $\frac{1}{3}$ ☐ $\frac{3}{5}$ or $\frac{2}{3}$ ☐ $\frac{3}{8}$ or $\frac{1}{4}$ ☐

Which two fractions in each row are equal?

$\frac{1}{4}$ $\frac{3}{8}$ $\frac{4}{12}$ $\frac{3}{12}$ $\frac{7}{8}$ $\frac{5}{8}$ ☐

$\frac{5}{8}$ $\frac{6}{9}$ $\frac{7}{10}$ $\frac{8}{12}$ $\frac{1}{2}$ $\frac{3}{4}$ ☐

$\frac{7}{12}$ $\frac{6}{14}$ $\frac{7}{14}$ $\frac{3}{8}$ $\frac{4}{8}$ $\frac{9}{12}$ ☐

$\frac{3}{8}$ $\frac{3}{9}$ $\frac{2}{6}$ $\frac{4}{7}$ $\frac{9}{10}$ $\frac{6}{7}$ ☐

$\frac{3}{10}$ $\frac{5}{15}$ $\frac{2}{10}$ $\frac{3}{15}$ $\frac{4}{10}$ $\frac{7}{15}$ ☐

Put these fractions in order starting with the smallest.

$\frac{1}{2}$ $\frac{5}{6}$ $\frac{2}{3}$ ☐

$\frac{5}{8}$ $\frac{3}{4}$ $\frac{11}{12}$ ☐

$\frac{2}{3}$ $\frac{8}{15}$ $\frac{3}{5}$ ☐

Converting fractions to decimals

Convert these fractions to decimals.

$$\frac{3}{10} = \boxed{0.3}$$

(because the three goes in the tenths column)

$$\frac{7}{100} = \boxed{0.07}$$

(because the seven goes in the hundredths column)

Convert these fractions to decimals.

$\frac{6}{10} =$ ⬚ $\frac{9}{100} =$ ⬚ $\frac{4}{100} =$ ⬚ $\frac{6}{100} =$ ⬚

$\frac{4}{10} =$ ⬚ $\frac{2}{10} =$ ⬚ $\frac{1}{10} =$ ⬚ $\frac{7}{100} =$ ⬚

$\frac{8}{100} =$ ⬚ $\frac{5}{10} =$ ⬚ $\frac{7}{10} =$ ⬚ $\frac{8}{10} =$ ⬚

$\frac{2}{100} =$ ⬚ $\frac{5}{100} =$ ⬚ $\frac{1}{100} =$ ⬚ $\frac{3}{10} =$ ⬚

Convert $\frac{1}{4}$ to a decimal.

To do this we have to divide the bottom number into the top.

When we run out of numbers we put in the decimal point and enough noughts to finish the sum. Be careful to keep the decimal point in your answer above the decimal point in the sum.

$$\begin{array}{r} 0.25 \\ 4\overline{)1.00} \end{array}$$

Convert these fractions to decimals.

$\frac{1}{2} =$ ⬚ $\frac{3}{4} =$ ⬚ $\frac{2}{5} =$ ⬚ $\frac{1}{5} =$ ⬚

$\frac{4}{5} =$ ⬚ $\frac{3}{8} =$ ⬚ $\frac{3}{5} =$ ⬚ $\frac{1}{4} =$ ⬚

Addition

Work out the answer to each sum.

```
    634              1 472
  4 812                 96
+ 1 428              8 391
─────────          +   564
  6 874            ─────────
   1   1            10 523
                      1  31
```

Remember to carry if you need to.

Work out the answer to each sum.

```
  5 831            3 724            9 994              524
  8 375            9 942            7 358            7 034
+   219          +   623          +   471          +    95
─────────        ─────────        ─────────        ─────────
```

```
  7 341            9 328            7 159              208
    299              347               39            4 943
+ 5 143          + 8 222          +   748          +    55
─────────        ─────────        ─────────        ─────────
```

Work out the answer to each sum.

```
  8 594            7 362            3 041            7 641
    629              843              571               93
  9 878            4 732            5 210            8 521
+    96          +    53          +    71          +   843
─────────        ─────────        ─────────        ─────────
```

```
  8 795            6 043               27              146
    659                4              153            3 714
  3 212              147            8 612               26
+   961          + 8 948          +   127          + 5 003
─────────        ─────────        ─────────        ─────────
```

More addition

Work out the answer to each sum.

```
   23 714          11 541
    9 024             861
 +    348          29 652
 ┌─────────┐    +       5
 │ 33 086  │    ┌─────────┐
 └─────────┘    │ 42 059  │
    1 1   1     └─────────┘
                   12  1
```

Remember to carry if you need to.

Work out the answer to each sum.

```
   17 203          29 521          65 214          25 046
      112           6 211             973              15
 +  5 608        +     58        +  1 291        +    263
 ┌───────┐      ┌───────┐       ┌───────┐       ┌───────┐
 └───────┘      └───────┘       └───────┘       └───────┘
```

```
    6 958          73 009          11 536          87 019
       71               3              48             127
 + 16 911        +    581        +  2 435        +  5 652
 ┌───────┐      ┌───────┐       ┌───────┐       ┌───────┐
 └───────┘      └───────┘       └───────┘       └───────┘
```

Work out the answer to each sum.

```
   79 622          64 599           6 940          72 148
    8 011             122             936             999
   47 391           6 375          58 274           7 481
 +      7        +      91        +      36        + 21 685
 ┌───────┐      ┌───────┐       ┌───────┐       ┌───────┐
 └───────┘      └───────┘       └───────┘       └───────┘
```

```
   58 975          36 403               8              23
      858              73          22 849          99 951
    8 423             712             502             358
 +     27        +  6 229        +  4 034        +  6 231
 ┌───────┐      ┌───────┐       ┌───────┐       ┌───────┐
 └───────┘      └───────┘       └───────┘       └───────┘
```

Subtraction

Work out the answer to each sum.

$$\begin{array}{r} 7\,^{1}31 \\ 8\cancel{4}3 \\ -\ \ 64 \\ \hline 779 \end{array} \qquad \begin{array}{r} 6\,^{1}11 \\ 4\ 7\cancel{2}1 \\ -\ \ 287 \\ \hline 4\ 434 \end{array}$$

Work out the answer to each sum.

$$\begin{array}{r} 635 \\ -\ 76 \\ \hline \end{array} \qquad \begin{array}{r} 812 \\ -\ 53 \\ \hline \end{array} \qquad \begin{array}{r} 937 \\ -\ 38 \\ \hline \end{array} \qquad \begin{array}{r} 528 \\ -\ 59 \\ \hline \end{array}$$

$$\begin{array}{r} 628 \\ -\ 29 \\ \hline \end{array} \qquad \begin{array}{r} 705 \\ -\ 76 \\ \hline \end{array} \qquad \begin{array}{r} 297 \\ -\ 58 \\ \hline \end{array} \qquad \begin{array}{r} 483 \\ -\ 94 \\ \hline \end{array}$$

$$\begin{array}{r} 854 \\ -\ 65 \\ \hline \end{array} \qquad \begin{array}{r} 362 \\ -\ 75 \\ \hline \end{array} \qquad \begin{array}{r} 963 \\ -\ 79 \\ \hline \end{array} \qquad \begin{array}{r} 248 \\ -\ 89 \\ \hline \end{array}$$

$$\begin{array}{r} 537 \\ -\ 78 \\ \hline \end{array} \qquad \begin{array}{r} 258 \\ -\ 69 \\ \hline \end{array} \qquad \begin{array}{r} 461 \\ -\ 77 \\ \hline \end{array} \qquad \begin{array}{r} 322 \\ -\ 39 \\ \hline \end{array}$$

Write the answer in the box.

$$317 - 49 = \qquad \qquad 286 - 98 =$$

$$423 - 85 = \qquad \qquad 176 - 87 =$$

Larry has 221 marbles. The lid comes off his tin and he loses 57. How many does he have left?

A school tuck shop has 537 packets of crisps. If they sell 69 packets how many are left?

More subtraction

Work out the answer to each sum.

$$\begin{array}{r} {}^{2}\,{}^{0}\,{}^{1}\,{}^{4\,1} \\ \cancel{3\ 1\cancel{5}4} \\ -\quad 665 \\ \hline \boxed{2\ 489} \end{array}$$

$$\begin{array}{r} {}^{2}\ {}^{1}\,{}^{5\,1} \\ 2\ \cancel{3}\cancel{6}1 \\ -\quad 72 \\ \hline \boxed{2\ 289} \end{array}$$

Work out the answer to each sum.

5 743	6 341	5 642	8 235
− 844	− 756	− 683	− 436

6 484	1 257	2 354	2 368
− 786	− 458	− 365	− 289

5 323	3 641	2 833	6 321
− 555	− 482	− 954	− 632

7 412	8 236	5 423	3 741
− 63	− 58	− 74	− 82

5 213	7 391	4 822	1 765
− 84	− 94	− 66	− 87

At a pop concert 865 programmes are sold. If 2 345 people are at the concert how many do not have programmes?

A bakery makes 6 243 loaves. If 455 loaves are returned unsold, how many were sold?

Subtraction with two zeros on top

Work out the answer to each sum.

$$\begin{array}{r} {}^{4}\cancel{5}{}^{9}\cancel{0}{}^{11}0 \\ -\quad 94 \\ \hline 406 \end{array}$$

$$\begin{array}{r} {}^{1}\cancel{2}{}^{9}\cancel{7}{}^{16}\cancel{0}{}^{11}0 \\ -\quad 927 \\ \hline 1\ 773 \end{array}$$

Work out the answer to each sum.

700 − 84	100 − 61	300 − 29	200 − 76
800 − 223	900 − 364	400 − 295	500 − 173
400 − 235	900 − 741	800 − 382	600 − 253
7 600 − 599	6 400 − 324	5 200 − 168	9 100 − 138
8 200 − 323	5 400 − 749	6 300 − 416	8 100 − 591
7 500 − 562	9 300 − 359	8 200 − 274	5 300 − 833
6 400 − 749	9 200 − 362	4 700 − 643	6 600 − 821

Real life problems

A ship sails 526 km to port A and then 753 km to port B. What is the total distance travelled?

1279 kilometres

```
  526
+ 753
 1279
```

In a sponsored walk, Sam and Karen walked a combined distance of 19 642 metres. If Karen walked 9 476 metres how far did Sam walk?

10 166 metres

```
   5 13 1
 19 642
- 9 476
 10 166
```

Kerry and Sean both make model cars. Kerry's is 65.42 cm long and Sean's is 24.87 cm long. What is the difference in length between their cars?

A sofa costs £845. A table costs £464. How much more is the sofa than the table?

Mr Bonner earns £19 426 per year.
Mrs Bonner earns £24 348 per year. Their daughter Kristy earns £742 a year from her paper round.

What is the total income of the family?

How much more would Kristy need to earn in order to get as much as her mother?

What is the difference between Mr and Mrs Bonner's income?

If Mrs Bonner gave up work, how much money would the family have per year?

Real life problems

A plumber has 6 m of copper tubing. If he uses
2.36 m, how much will he have left?

3.64 m

```
      5 ₁9 ₁
      6.00
    − 2.36
      3.64
```

If he buys another 4.5 m of copper tubing,
how much will he now have?

8.14 m

```
      3.64
    + 4.50
      8.14
       ₁
```

A man spends £35.65, £102.43, £68.99 and
£36.50 in 4 different shops. How much did he
spend altogether?

A petrol station has 10 400 litres of petrol delivered on Monday,
13 350 litres on Tuesday, 14 755 litres on Wednesday, 9 656 litres
on Thursday, and 15 975 litres on Friday. How much did they
have delivered from Monday to Friday?

If they sold 59 248 litres,
how much petrol did
they have left?

Daniel runs 22.56 km in a charity fun run.
Sandra runs 8 420 m less.
How far does Sandra run?

What is the combined distance
run by Daniel and Sandra?

Dianne is 1.61 m tall. Her friend is 1.8 m tall.
How much taller is Dianne's friend?

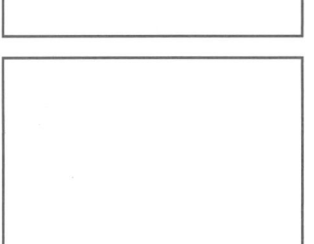

13

Real life problems

A man walks 18.34 km on Saturday and 16.57 km on Sunday.
How far did he walk that weekend?

34.91 km

How much further did he walk on Saturday?

1.77 km

$$
\begin{array}{r}
18.34 \\
+16.57 \\
\hline
34.91 \\
\end{array}
$$

$$
\begin{array}{r}
18.34 \\
-16.57 \\
\hline
1.77 \\
\end{array}
$$

A rectangular field measures 103.7 m
by 96.5 m. How long is the perimeter
of the field?

When Joe and Kerry stand on a weighing machine
it reads 136.53 kg. When Joe steps off, it reads
68.76 kg. How much does Joe weigh?

A rectangular room has an area of 32.58 m².
When a carpet is put down there is still 7.99 m²
of floor showing. What is the area of the carpet?

A brother and sister's combined height is
3.27 m. If the sister is 1.59 m tall, how tall
is the brother?

A country has 4 motorways, the MA which is 1 246 km long,
the MB which is 339 km long, the MC which is 1 573 km
long, and the MD which is 48 km long. How much motorway
does the country have in total?

Jenny's aquarium holds 25.56 litres of
water. She buys a new one which holds
32 litres. How much extra water do her
fish have?

14

Simple use of brackets

Work out these sums.

$(4 + 6) - (2 + 1) =$ $10 - 3 = 7$

$(2 \times 5) + (10 - 4) =$ $10 + 6 = 16$

Remember to work out the brackets first.

Work out these sums.

$(5 + 3) + (6 - 2) =$

$(6 - 1) - (1 + 2) =$

$(8 + 3) + (12 - 2) =$

$(7 - 2) + (4 + 5) =$

$(3 - 1) + (12 - 1) =$

$(9 + 5) - (3 + 6) =$

$(14 + 12) - (9 + 4) =$

$(9 - 3) - (4 + 2) =$

Now try these longer sums.

$(5 + 9) + (12 - 2) - (4 + 3) =$

$(10 + 5) - (2 + 4) + (9 + 6) =$

$(19 + 4) - (3 + 2) - (2 + 1) =$

$(24 - 5) - (3 + 7) - (5 - 2) =$

$(15 + 3) + (7 - 2) - (5 + 7) =$

Now try these. Be careful, the brackets now have multiplication sums.

$(2 \times 3) + (5 \times 2) =$

$(7 \times 2) + (3 \times 3) =$

$(6 \times 4) - (4 \times 3) =$

$(12 \times 4) - (8 \times 3) =$

$(3 \times 4) - (2 \times 2) =$

$(5 \times 4) - (3 \times 2) =$

$(9 \times 5) - (4 \times 6) =$

$(7 \times 4) - (8 \times 2) =$

If the answer is 24, which of these sums gives the correct answer? Write the letter in the box.

a $(3 + 5) + (3 \times 1)$

b $(3 \times 5) + (3 \times 2)$

c $(3 \times 5) + (3 \times 3)$

d $(2 \times 5) + (2 \times 6)$

e $(5 \times 7) - (2 \times 5)$

f $(6 + 7) + (12 - 2)$

Simple use of brackets

Work out these sums.

$(7 + 3) \quad \times \quad (8 - 4) =$ ⬜ $(5 - 2) \quad \times \quad (8 - 1) =$ ⬜

$(9 + 5) \quad \div \quad (1 + 6) =$ ⬜ $(14 - 6) \quad \times \quad (4 + 3) =$ ⬜

$(14 + 4) \div (12 - 6) =$ ⬜ $(9 + 21) \div (8 - 5) =$ ⬜

$(11 - 5) \quad \times \quad (7 + 5) =$ ⬜ $(8 + 20) \div (12 - 10) =$ ⬜

$(6 + 9) \quad \div \quad (8 - 3) =$ ⬜ $(14 - 3) \quad \times \quad (6 + 1) =$ ⬜

$(10 + 10) \div (2 + 3) =$ ⬜ $(9 + 3) \quad \times \quad (2 + 4) =$ ⬜

Now try these.

$(4 \times 3) \quad \div \quad (1 \times 2) =$ ⬜ $(5 \times 4) \quad \div \quad (2 \times 2) =$ ⬜

$(8 \times 5) \quad \div \quad (4 \times 1) =$ ⬜ $(6 \times 4) \quad \div \quad (3 \times 4) =$ ⬜

$(2 \times 4) \quad \times \quad (2 \times 3) =$ ⬜ $(3 \times 5) \quad \times \quad (1 \times 2) =$ ⬜

$(8 \times 4) \quad \div \quad (2 \times 2) =$ ⬜ $(6 \times 4) \quad \div \quad (4 \times 2) =$ ⬜

If the answer is 30, which of these sums gives the correct answer?

a $(3 \times 5) \times (2 \times 2)$ d $(20 \div 2) \times (12 \div 3)$

b $(4 \times 5) \times (5 \times 2)$ e $(5 \times 12) \div (2 \times 5)$

c $(12 \times 5) \div (8 \div 4)$ f $(9 \times 5) \div (10 \div 2)$ ⬜

If the answer is 8, which of these sums gives the correct answer?

a $(16 \div 2) \div (2 \times 1)$ d $(24 \div 6) \times (8 \div 4)$

b $(9 \div 3) \times (3 \times 2)$ e $(8 \div 4) \times (8 \div 1)$

c $(12 \times 4) \div (6 \times 2)$ f $(16 \div 4) \times (20 \div 4)$ ⬜

Simple use of brackets

Work out these sums.

$(5 + 3) + (9 - 2) =$ $8 + 7 = 15$

$(5 + 2) - (4 - 1) =$ $7 - 3 = 4$

$(4 \times 5) \times (3 + 1) =$ $6 \times 4 = 24$

$(3 \times 5) \div (9 - 6) =$ $15 \div 3 = 5$

Remember to work out the brackets first.

Work out these sums.

$(5 + 4) + (7 - 3) =$ $(9 - 2) + (6 + 4) =$

$(7 + 3) - (9 - 7) =$ $(15 - 5) + (2 + 3) =$

$(11 \times 2) - (3 \times 2) =$ $(15 \div 3) + (9 \times 2) =$

$(12 \times 2) - (3 \times 3) =$ $(6 \div 2) + (8 \times 2) =$

$(9 \times 3) - (7 \times 3) =$ $(15 \div 5) + (3 \times 4) =$

$(20 \div 5) - (8 \div 2) =$ $(5 \times 10) - (12 \times 4) =$

Now try these.

$(4 + 8) \div (3 \times 2) =$ $(6 \times 4) \div (3 \times 2) =$

$(9 + 5) \div (2 \times 1) =$ $(7 \times 4) \div (3 + 4) =$

$(3 + 6) \times (3 \times 3) =$ $(5 \times 5) \div (10 \div 2) =$

$(24 \div 2) \times (3 \times 2) =$ $(8 \times 6) \div (2 \times 12) =$

Write down the letters of all the sums that make 25.

a $(2 \times 5) \times (3 \times 2)$ d $(40 \div 2) + (10 \div 2)$

b $(5 \times 5) + (7 - 2)$ e $(10 \times 5) - (5 \times 5)$

c $(6 \times 5) - (10 \div 2)$ f $(10 \times 10) \div (10 - 6)$

Write down the letters of all the sums that make 20.

a $(10 \div 2) \times (4 \div 4)$ d $(20 \div 4) \times (8 + 2)$

b $(7 \times 3) - (3 \div 3)$ e $(10 \div 2) + (20 \div 2)$

c $(8 \times 4) - (6 \times 2)$ f $(14 \div 2) + (2 \times 7)$

Multiplying decimals

Work out these sums.

$$\begin{array}{r} 4.6 \\ \times\ \ 3 \\ \hline 13.8 \\ \hline \end{array} \qquad \begin{array}{r} 3.9 \\ \times\ \ 5 \\ \hline 19.5 \\ \hline \end{array} \qquad \begin{array}{r} 8.4 \\ \times\ \ 8 \\ \hline 67.2 \\ \hline \end{array}$$

1   4   3

Work out these sums.

$$\begin{array}{r} 4.7 \\ \times\ \ 3 \\ \hline \end{array} \qquad \begin{array}{r} 9.1 \\ \times\ \ 3 \\ \hline \end{array} \qquad \begin{array}{r} 5.8 \\ \times\ \ 3 \\ \hline \end{array} \qquad \begin{array}{r} 1.7 \\ \times\ \ 2 \\ \hline \end{array} \qquad \begin{array}{r} 5.1 \\ \times\ \ 2 \\ \hline \end{array}$$

$$\begin{array}{r} 7.4 \\ \times\ \ 2 \\ \hline \end{array} \qquad \begin{array}{r} 3.6 \\ \times\ \ 4 \\ \hline \end{array} \qquad \begin{array}{r} 6.5 \\ \times\ \ 4 \\ \hline \end{array} \qquad \begin{array}{r} 4.2 \\ \times\ \ 2 \\ \hline \end{array} \qquad \begin{array}{r} 3.8 \\ \times\ \ 2 \\ \hline \end{array}$$

$$\begin{array}{r} 4.2 \\ \times\ \ 4 \\ \hline \end{array} \qquad \begin{array}{r} 4.7 \\ \times\ \ 4 \\ \hline \end{array} \qquad \begin{array}{r} 1.8 \\ \times\ \ 5 \\ \hline \end{array} \qquad \begin{array}{r} 3.4 \\ \times\ \ 5 \\ \hline \end{array} \qquad \begin{array}{r} 3.7 \\ \times\ \ 5 \\ \hline \end{array}$$

$$\begin{array}{r} 2.5 \\ \times\ \ 5 \\ \hline \end{array} \qquad \begin{array}{r} 2.4 \\ \times\ \ 6 \\ \hline \end{array} \qquad \begin{array}{r} 5.3 \\ \times\ \ 7 \\ \hline \end{array} \qquad \begin{array}{r} 7.2 \\ \times\ \ 8 \\ \hline \end{array} \qquad \begin{array}{r} 5.1 \\ \times\ \ 9 \\ \hline \end{array}$$

$$\begin{array}{r} 7.9 \\ \times\ \ 9 \\ \hline \end{array} \qquad \begin{array}{r} 8.6 \\ \times\ \ 9 \\ \hline \end{array} \qquad \begin{array}{r} 8.8 \\ \times\ \ 8 \\ \hline \end{array} \qquad \begin{array}{r} 7.5 \\ \times\ \ 8 \\ \hline \end{array} \qquad \begin{array}{r} 9.9 \\ \times\ \ 6 \\ \hline \end{array}$$

$$\begin{array}{r} 6.8 \\ \times\ \ 7 \\ \hline \end{array} \qquad \begin{array}{r} 5.7 \\ \times\ \ 6 \\ \hline \end{array} \qquad \begin{array}{r} 6.9 \\ \times\ \ 7 \\ \hline \end{array} \qquad \begin{array}{r} 7.5 \\ \times\ \ 9 \\ \hline \end{array} \qquad \begin{array}{r} 8.4 \\ \times\ \ 9 \\ \hline \end{array}$$

$$\begin{array}{r} 7.3 \\ \times\ \ 8 \\ \hline \end{array} \qquad \begin{array}{r} 2.8 \\ \times\ \ 7 \\ \hline \end{array} \qquad \begin{array}{r} 3.8 \\ \times\ \ 8 \\ \hline \end{array} \qquad \begin{array}{r} 7.7 \\ \times\ \ 7 \\ \hline \end{array} \qquad \begin{array}{r} 9.4 \\ \times\ \ 9 \\ \hline \end{array}$$

Multiplying decimals

Work out these sums.

37.5	26.2	65.3
x 2	x 5	x 9
75.0	**131.0**	**587.7**
1 1	3 1	4 2

Work out these sums.

| 53.3 | 93.2 | 51.4 | 34.6 | 35.2 |
| x   2 | x   2 | x   2 | x   3 | x   3 |

| 46.5 | 25.8 | 16.4 | 47.1 | 37.4 |
| x   4 | x   4 | x   3 | x   5 | x   5 |

| 12.4 | 46.3 | 17.5 | 36.5 | 72.4 |
| x   5 | x   5 | x   6 | x   6 | x   7 |

| 37.5 | 20.3 | 73.4 | 92.6 | 47.9 |
| x   7 | x   7 | x   7 | x   6 | x   6 |

| 53.9 | 75.6 | 28.8 | 79.4 | 99.9 |
| x   8 | x   8 | x   8 | x   8 | x   9 |

| 37.9 | 14.8 | 35.4 | 46.8 | 27.2 |
| x   9 | x   9 | x   9 | x   8 | x   7 |

| 39.5 | 84.2 | 68.5 | 73.2 | 47.6 |
| x   6 | x   9 | x   8 | x   9 | x   6 |

Real life problems

Nigel earns £1.50 a day on his paper round.
How much does he earn per week?

£10.50

$$\begin{array}{r} £1.50 \\ \times \quad 7 \\ \hline £10.50 \\ \hline 3 \end{array}$$

When Ivan subtracts the width of his cupboard
from the length of his bedroom wall he finds he
has 3.65 m of wall space left. If the cupboard is
0.87 m wide, what is the length of his bedroom wall?

4.52 m

$$\begin{array}{r} 3.65 \text{ m} \\ +0.87 \text{ m} \\ \hline 4.52 \text{ m} \\ \hline 1 \ 1 \end{array}$$

Sophie buys her mother a bunch of flowers
for £12.95 and her brothers some sweets for
£2.76. If she has £7.83 left how much did
she start with?

If David were 7.5 cm taller, he would be
twice as tall as Ian. Ian is 74.25 cm tall,
so how tall is David?

Stanley is making some shelves which are
75.5 cm long. If the wood he is using is
180 cm long, how many pieces will he need
to make six shelves?

A café uses 27.5 litres of milk a day. If they
have a weekly delivery of 180 litres, how
much will they have left after six days?

Charles has 12.5 m of railway track. Gavin
has 8.6 m and Kristy has 4.8 m. If they put
their track together how long will their
circuit be?

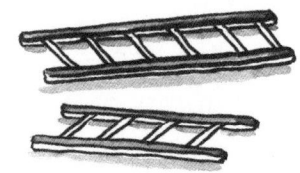

Real life problems

A novelist writes 9.5 pages of his book each day.
How many pages will he write in 9 days?

85.5 pages

```
    9.5
x     9
   85.5
      4
```

After driving 147.75 km a driver stops
at a service station. If he has another
115.43 km to go, how long will his journey be?

263.18 km

```
  147.75
+ 115.43
  263.18
    1 1
```

Mr Mayfield divides his money equally
among four separate banks. If he has £98.65
in each bank, what is the total of his savings?

Mrs Eldon buys 2 bottles of perfume; one contains
48.5 ml and the other contains 150.5 ml. How much
more perfume is in the larger of the two bottles?

A teacher spends 5.75 minutes marking
each story. How long would it take to
mark 8 stories?

8 tiles each 15.75 cm wide fit exactly across
the width of the bathroom wall. How wide is
the bathroom wall?

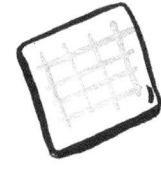

Terry has £8.50. If he spends £1.05 a day
over the next seven days, how much will he
have left at the end of the seven days?

A shop sells 427.56 kg of loose peanuts the
first week and 246.94 kg the second week.
How much did they sell over the two weeks?

Real life problems

In a class of 30 children 6 children are painting.
What percentage of children are painting?
$\frac{6}{30}$ of the children are painting
and to change a fraction to
a percentage we multiply by 100.

20%

$$\frac{6}{30} \times 100 = 20$$

40% of a class is made up of girls. If there are
12 girls, how many children are in the class?
If 12 girls are 40% of the class, we
divide 12 by 40 to find 1%.
Then we multiply by 100 to find 100%.

30 children

$$\frac{12}{40} \times 100 = 30$$

A shop has 60 books by a new author. If it sells
45 of the books what percentage does it sell?

A school disco sells 65% of its tickets. If it had
120 tickets to start with, how many has it sold?

200 people go on a school trip. If 14% are
adults, how many children go on the trip?

A shop sells 150 T-shirts but 12 are returned
because they are faulty. What percentage of
the T-shirts was faulty?

A year group of 120 children are asked their
favourite colours.

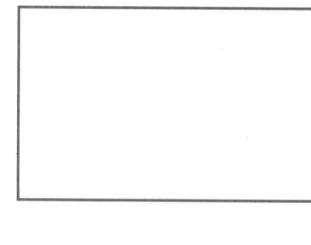

15% like red. How many children like red?

20% like green. How many children like green?

30% like yellow. How many children like yellow?

35% like blue. How many children like blue?

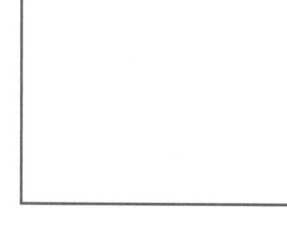

Real life problems

Deborah's school bag weighs 4.67 kg.
Asha's weighs 3.98 kg. How much more does
Deborah's weigh than Asha's?

0.69 kg

What is the total weight of the two bags?

8.65 kg

```
  3 ¹5 1
  4.̶6̶7
−  3.98
   0.69
   4.67
+  3.98
   8.65
    1 1
```

A man wants to fit a new door. If the door frame
is 2m 5cm high and the new door is 2.09 m long,
how much will he have to cut off the door?

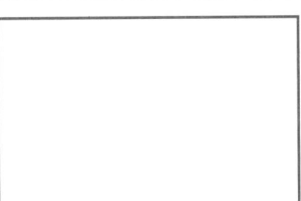

Bert earns £14 632 a year, George earns
£24 321 a year, and Horace earns £12 971
a year. How much do they earn altogether?

How much more than Bert
does George earn?

How much more than Horace does
Bert earn?

How much more than Horace does
George earn?

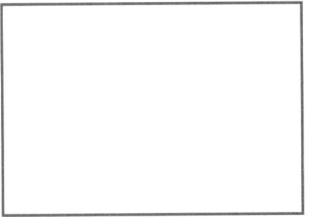

A lift says 'Maximum weight 270 kg'. If four people get
in weighing 72.93 kg, 47.81 kg, 85.99 kg, and 79.36 kg,
by how much are they overloading the lift?

Comparing units

Approximately how many centimetres are there in 5 inches?
There are approximately 2.5 cm to 1 inch.

| 12.5 cm |

$$\begin{array}{r} 2.5 \\ \times\ 5 \\ \hline 12.5 \end{array}$$

Approximately how many kilometres are there in 3 miles?
There are approximately 1.6 km in 1 mile.

| 4.8 km |

$$\begin{array}{r} 1.6 \\ \times\ 3 \\ \hline 4.8 \end{array}$$

Using the approximations in the example, convert these inches to centimetres.

| 2 inches | 4 inches | 3 inches | 7 inches |

| 6 inches | 10 inches | 9 inches | 8 inches |

Using the approximations in the example, convert these miles to kilometres.

| 2 miles | 5 miles | 4 miles | 8 miles |

| 10 miles | 6 miles | 7 miles | 9 miles |

Comparing units

Approximately how many pounds are there in 4 kg?
There are approximately 2.2 lb to 1 kg.

8.8 lb

```
    2.2
  ×   4
    8.8
```

Approximately how many litres are there in 5 pints?
A pint is approximately 0.6 of a litre.

3.0 litres

```
    0.6
  ×   5
    3.0
     3
```

Using the approximations in the example, convert these kilograms to pounds.

2 kg	6 kg	3 kg	7 kg
5 kg	9 kg	8 kg	10 kg

Using the approximations in the example, convert these pints to litres.

10 pints	8 pints	2 pints	4 pints
7 pints	9 pints	3 pints	6 pints

Naming parts of a circle

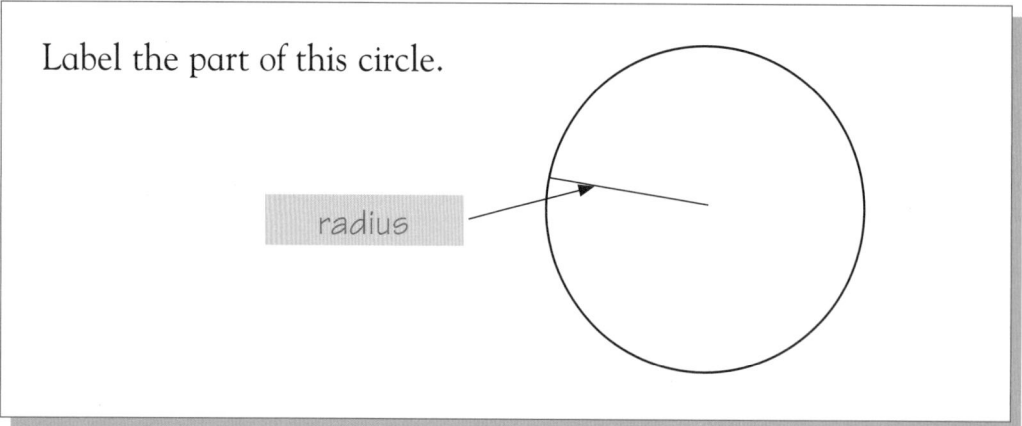

Label the part of this circle.

radius

Choose from the following words to label these circles:
radius, diameter, centre, arc, sector, quadrant

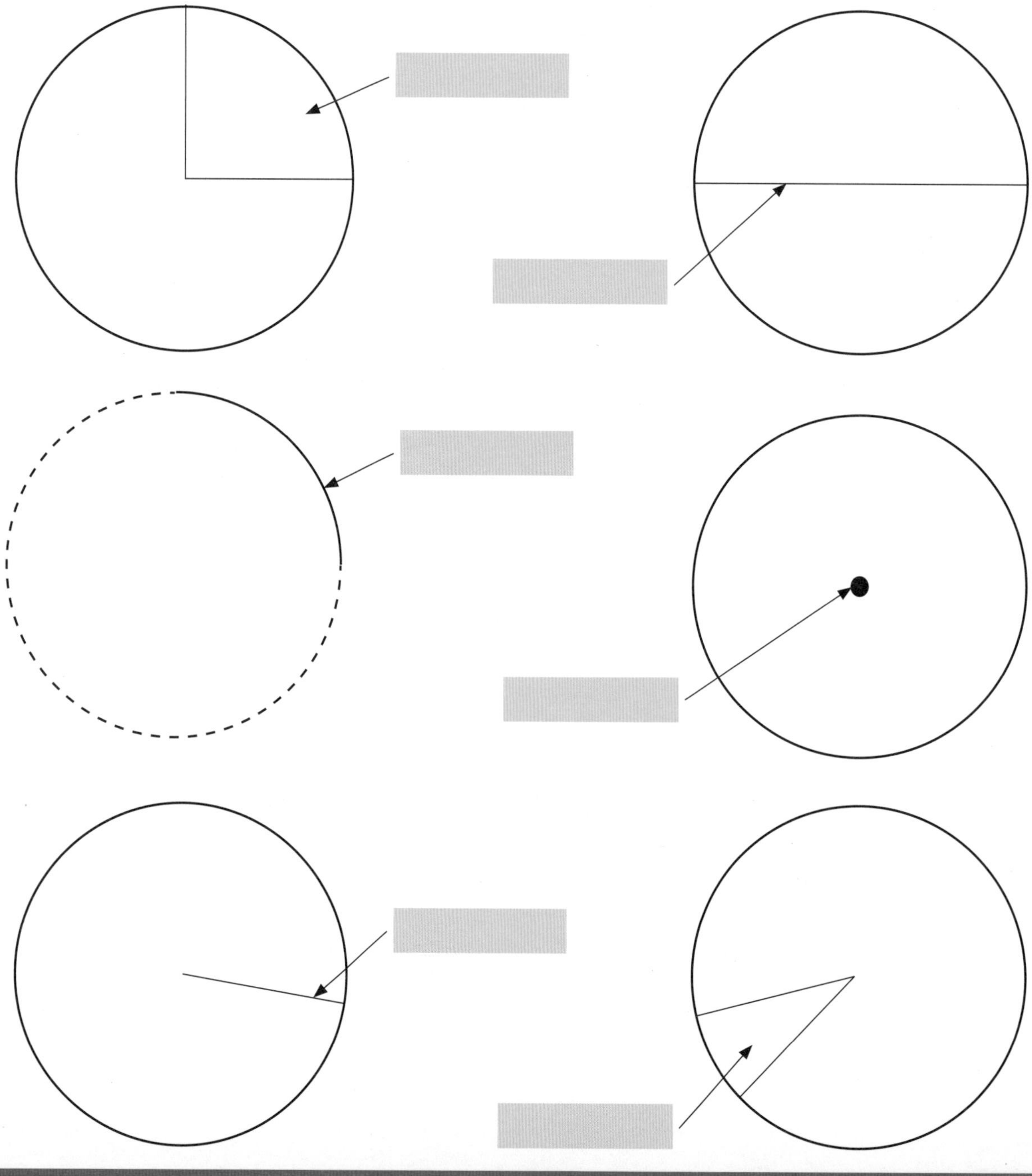

Area of right-angled triangles

Find the area of this right-angled triangle.

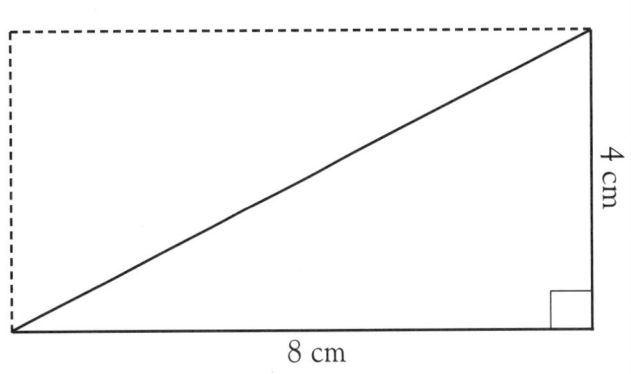

Because the area of this triangle is
half the area of the rectangle shown,
we can find the area of the rectangle and
then divide it by two to find the area
of the triangle.
So the area = (8 cm × 4 cm) ÷ 2
= 32 ÷ 2 = 16 cm²

Area = 16 cm²

Find the areas of these right-angled triangles.

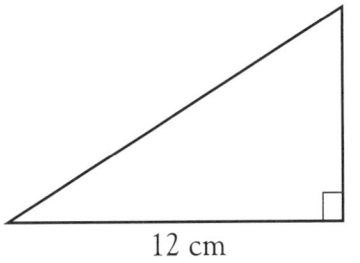

_____ cm²

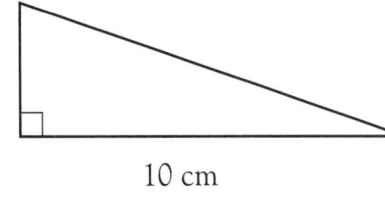

_____ cm²

_____ cm²

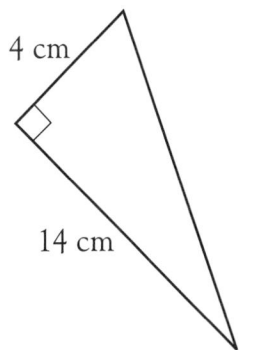

_____ cm²

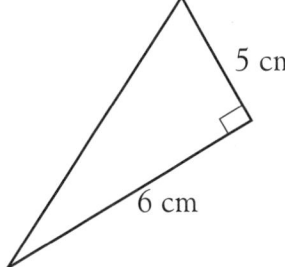

_____ cm²

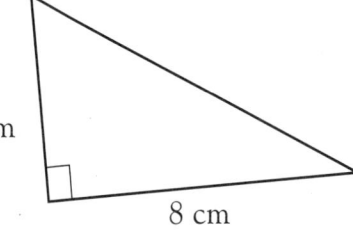

_____ cm²

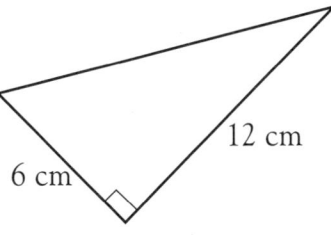

_____ cm²

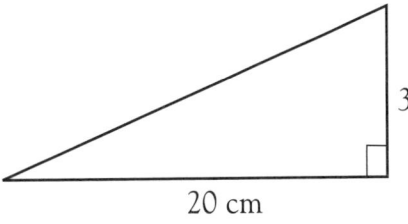

_____ cm²

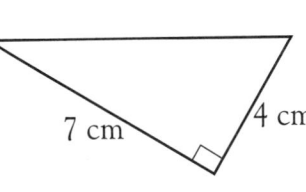

_____ cm²

Speed problems

How long would it take to travel
120 km at 8 kph?
(Time = Distance ÷ Speed)

15 hours

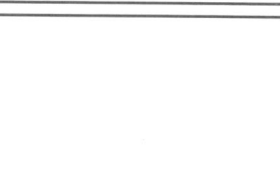

If a lorry takes 3 hours to travel 150 miles,
how fast is it going?
(Speed = Distance ÷ Time)

50 mph

If a car travels at 60 mph for 2 hours,
how far has it gone?
(Distance = Speed x Time)

120 miles

If a man walks for 3 kilometres at a
steady speed of 6 kph, how long will
it take him?

A lorry driver travels 120 km in 3 hours.
If he drove at a steady speed how fast
was he going?

A car travels at a steady speed of 90 kph.
How far will it travel in 4 hours?

Shane walks 8 miles at 2 mph.
Damien walks 9 miles at 3 mph.
Which of them will take the longest?

Courtney drives for 30 minutes at
50 mph and for 1 hour at 35 mph.
How far has he travelled altogether?

A racing car travels 35 miles in 30 minutes.
What speed is it travelling at?

Likely outcomes

Throw a coin 20 times.

Keep a tally.

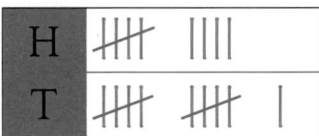

What do you notice?

Heads and tails come up roughly the same number of times because there are only two possible outcomes, and they are equally likely.

Put your results on a bar chart.

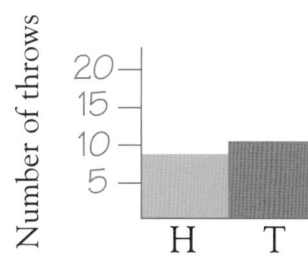

Predict what you think the outcome would be if you tossed two coins 48 times.

2 heads ⬚   2 tails ⬚   1 of each ⬚

Now throw two coins 48 times yourself and record your results on this tally chart.

2 Heads	
2 Tails	
1 of each	

Draw a bar chart to show your results.

Number of throws

50 45 40 35 30 25 20 15 10 5 0

Heads   Tails   1 of each

Which result comes up the most often?

Can you explain why some results are more probable than others?

Interpreting pie charts

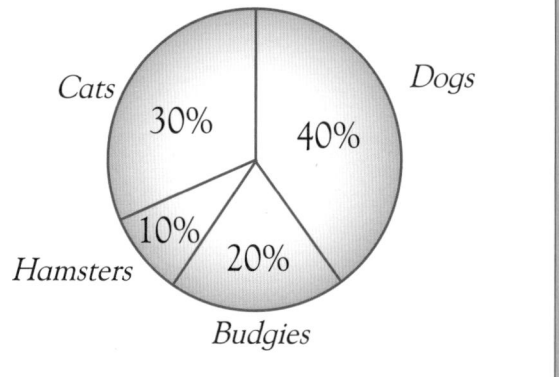

40 children voted for their favourite pet.
How many children prefer cats?
30% of 40 is 12

> 12 children

How many children prefer budgies?
20% of 40 is 8

> 8 children

A group of 60 children voted for their favourite author.

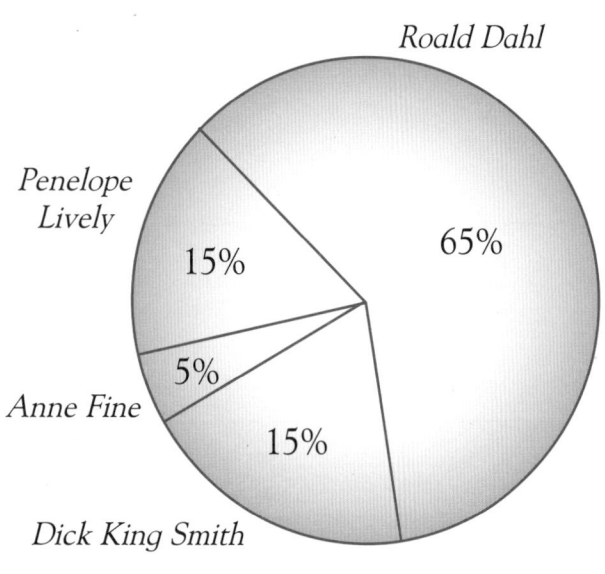

How many prefer Roald Dahl?

How many like either Penelope Lively
or Anne Fine?

How many children like either Penelope
Lively or Dick King Smith?

How many more children like Roald
Dahl than the other three together?

How many do not like Anne Fine?

80 children were asked what their hobbies were.
The pie chart shows the results.

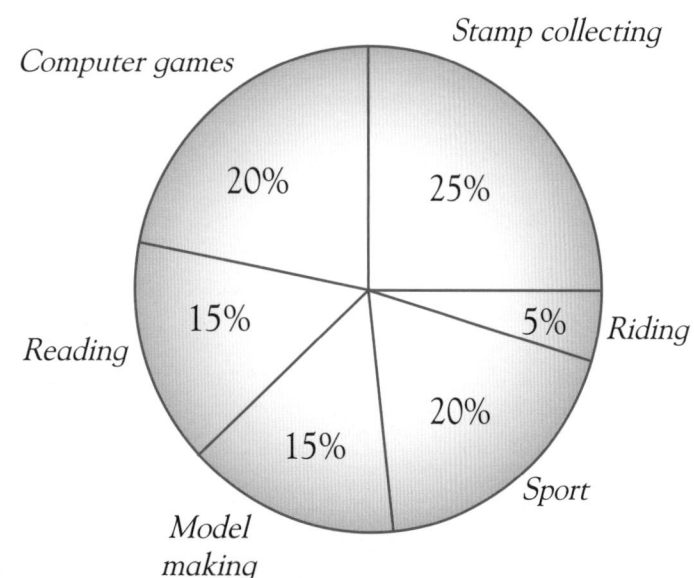

How many children like reading?

How many more children do sport than
make models?

How many children either read or collect
stamps for a hobby?

How many children do not like computer
games?

Interpreting pie charts

120 Year 6 children were surveyed to find out what type of home they lived in.

How many children lived in terraced houses?
20% of 120 is 24.

> 24 children

How many children lived in flats?
10% of 120 is 12.

> 12 children

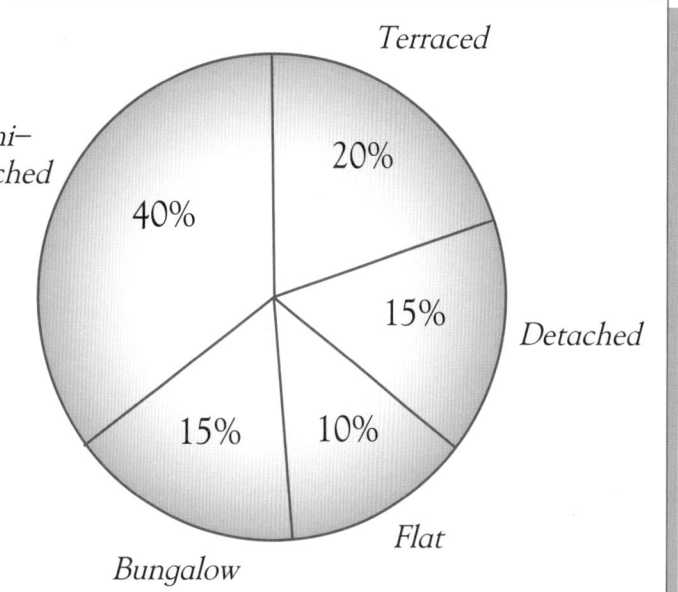

A group of 40 children recorded their eye colours.

How many had blue eyes?

How many had either hazel or green eyes?

How many more had brown eyes than grey?

How many did not have hazel eyes?

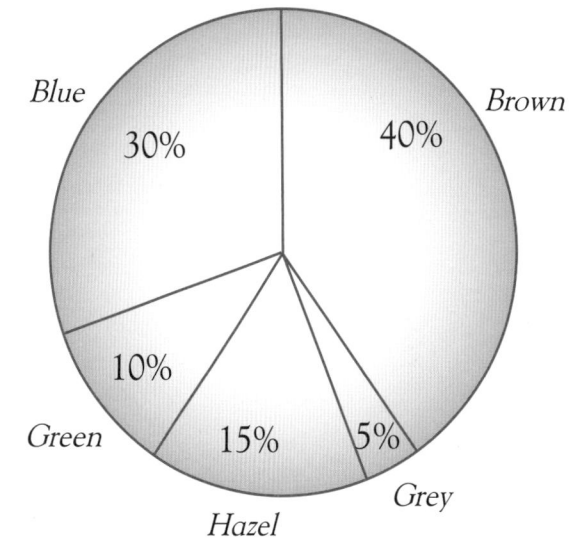

As part of a school project, Lar records the colours of 150 cars in his local supermarket's car park. He records his information on a pie chart.

How many blue cars were there?

How many yellow cars were there?

How many people did not drive a red car?

How many people did not drive green or white cars?

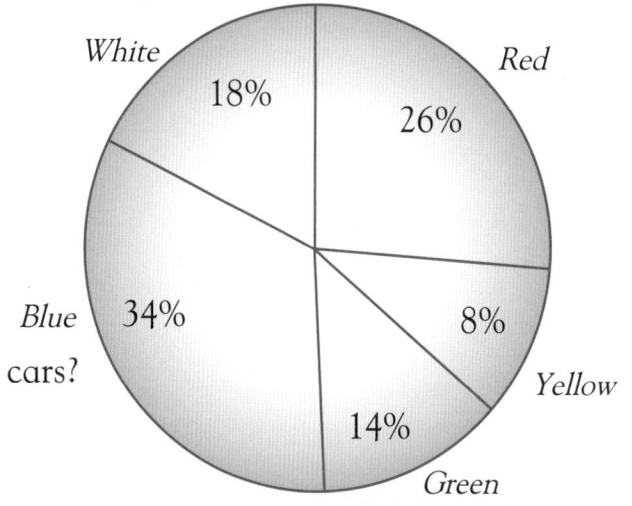

Drawing 2D shapes

Congruent shapes are shapes that have angles and sides of exactly the same size.

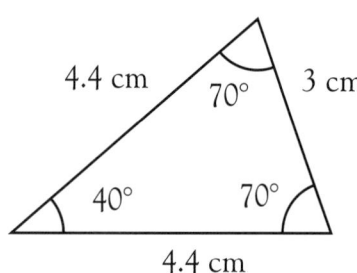 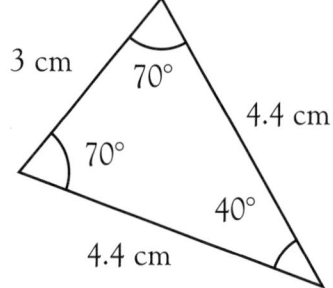

These shapes are congruent because they can be fitted exactly on top of each other.

Measure the angles and sides of these shapes and draw a congruent shape next to each one.

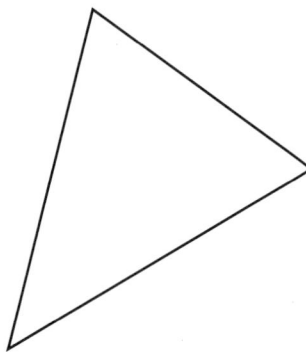 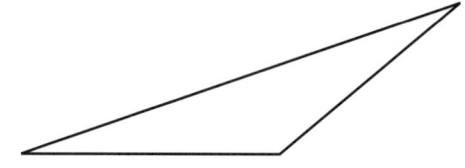

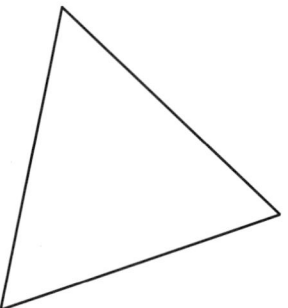 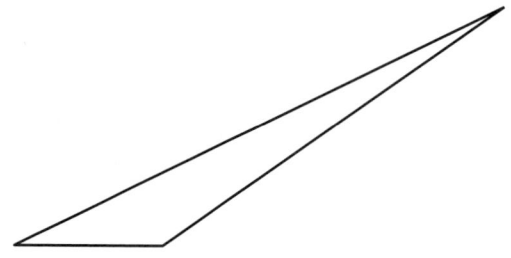

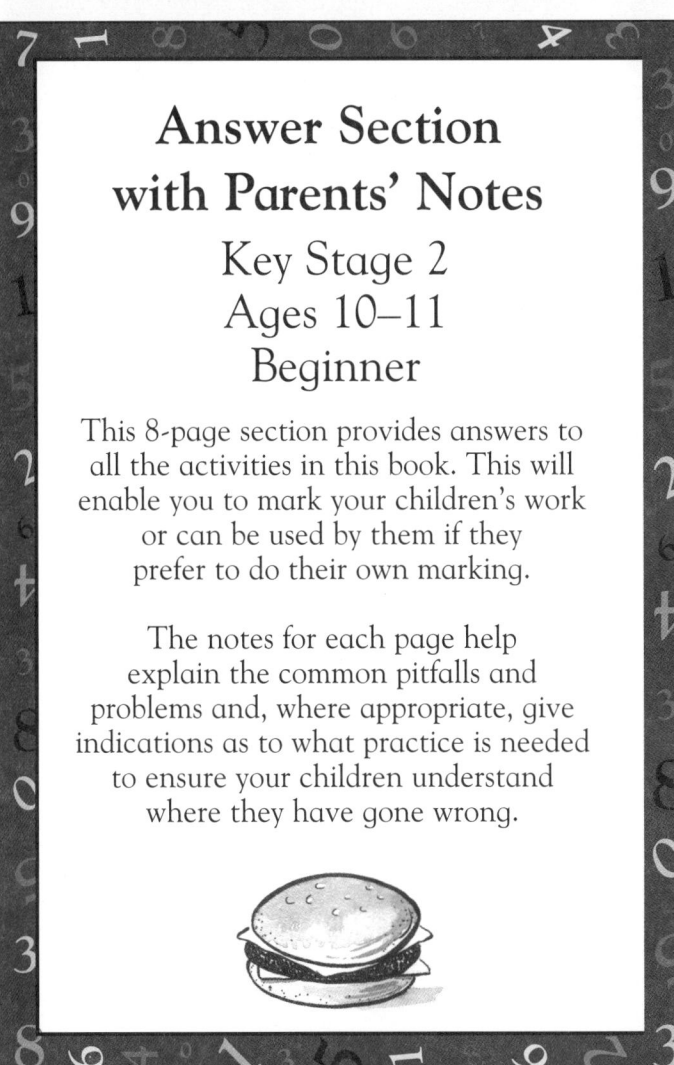

Answer Section with Parents' Notes

Key Stage 2
Ages 10–11
Beginner

This 8-page section provides answers to all the activities in this book. This will enable you to mark your children's work or can be used by them if they prefer to do their own marking.

The notes for each page help explain the common pitfalls and problems and, where appropriate, give indications as to what practice is needed to ensure your children understand where they have gone wrong.

Decimal addition

Write the answer to each sum.

296.48 + 131.74 **428.22**	173.05 + 269.23 **442.28**

Write the answer to each sum.

491.83 + 137.84 **629.67**	964.71 + 321.26 **1285.97**	302.04 + 204.99 **507.03**	306.25 + 844.24 **1150.49**
471.93 + 755.26 **1227.19**	842.01 + 711.84 **1553.85**	675.82 + 105.23 **781.05**	137.82 + 399.71 **537.53**
465.24 + 605.27 **1070.51**	178.93 + 599.41 **778.34**	184.74 + 372.81 **557.55**	443.27 + 705.99 **1149.26**
563.23 + 413.98 **977.21**	703.95 + 685.11 **1389.06**	825.36 + 249.85 **1075.21**	529.33 + 482.56 **1011.89**

Write the answer to each sum.

421.79 + 136.25 = **558.04**   192.31 + 241.73 = **434.04**

558.32 + 137.94 = **696.26**   501.84 + 361.93 = **863.77**

227.66 + 142.07 = **369.73**   275.31 + 239.33 = **514.64**

153.31 + 189.02 = **342.33**   491.44 + 105.37 = **596.81**

253.71 + 562.41 = **816.12**   829.25 + 163.74 = **992.99**

Look out for errors when the child is working horizontally, adding digits with different place values. Less confident children may need to be reassured when carrying across the decimal point.

Problems with negative numbers

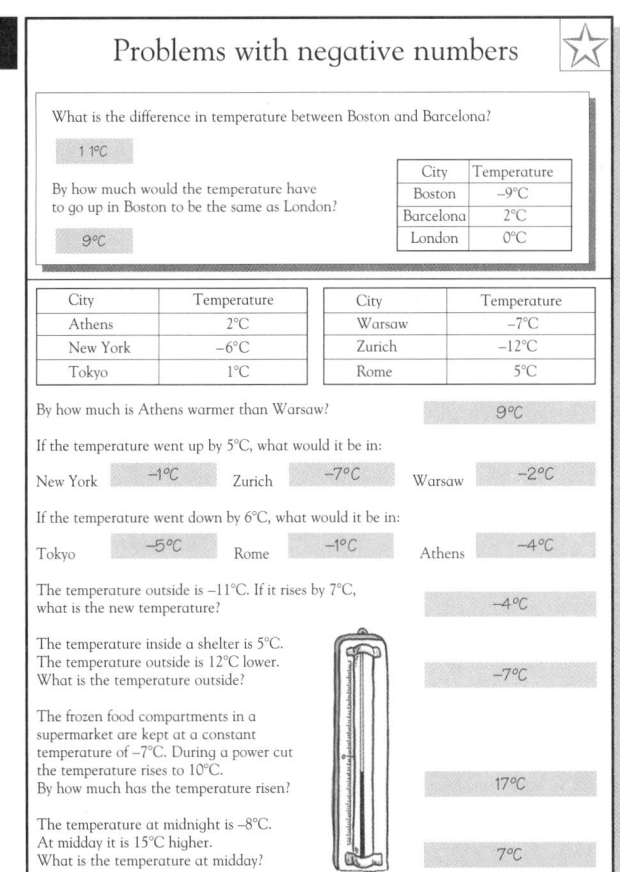

What is the difference in temperature between Boston and Barcelona?

11°C

By how much would the temperature have to go up in Boston to be the same as London?

9°C

City	Temperature
Boston	–9°C
Barcelona	2°C
London	0°C

City	Temperature		City	Temperature
Athens	2°C		Warsaw	–7°C
New York	–6°C		Zurich	–12°C
Tokyo	1°C		Rome	5°C

By how much is Athens warmer than Warsaw?   **9°C**

If the temperature went up by 5°C, what would it be in:

New York **–1°C**   Zurich **–7°C**   Warsaw **–2°C**

If the temperature went down by 6°C, what would it be in:

Tokyo **–5°C**   Rome **–1°C**   Athens **–4°C**

The temperature outside is –11°C. If it rises by 7°C, what is the new temperature?   **–4°C**

The temperature inside a shelter is 5°C. The temperature outside is 12°C lower. What is the temperature outside?   **–7°C**

The frozen food compartments in a supermarket are kept at a constant temperature of –7°C. During a power cut the temperature rises to 10°C. By how much has the temperature risen?   **17°C**

The temperature at midnight is –8°C. At midday it is 15°C higher. What is the temperature at midday?   **7°C**

When children add to, or subtract from, negative numbers they may have difficulty understanding why the number appears to get smaller when they add, and larger when they subtract. The use of a number line, e.g. a thermometer, makes the operation clearer.

Square roots

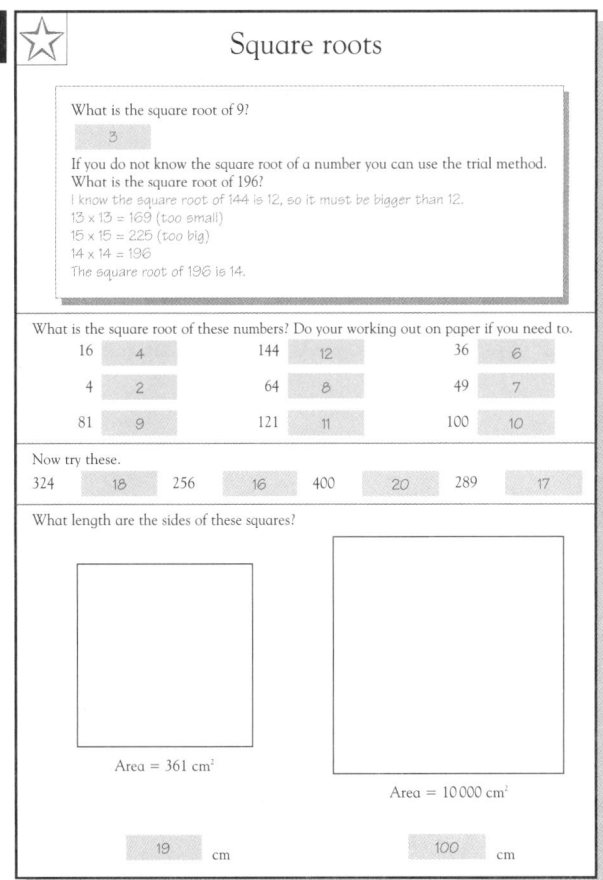

What is the square root of 9?

3

If you do not know the square root of a number you can use the trial method. What is the square root of 196?
I know the square root of 144 is 12, so it must be bigger than 12.
13 x 13 = 169 (too small)
15 x 15 = 225 (too big)
14 x 14 = 196
The square root of 196 is 14.

What is the square root of these numbers? Do your working out on paper if you need to.

16	**4**	144	**12**	36	**6**
4	**2**	64	**8**	49	**7**
81	**9**	121	**11**	100	**10**

Now try these.

324 **18**   256 **16**   400 **20**   289 **17**

What length are the sides of these squares?

Area = 361 cm²   **19** cm

Area = 10 000 cm²   **100** cm

Difficulty in the first section will highlight weaknesses in times tables knowledge. In the second and third sections, children should use the trial and improvement method outlined in the example.

Comparing fractions

Which is bigger, $\frac{2}{3}$ or $\frac{3}{4}$? $\boxed{\frac{3}{4}}$

The common denominator of 3 and 4 is 12.

So $\frac{2}{3} = \frac{8}{12}$ and $\frac{3}{4} = \frac{9}{12}$

$\frac{3}{4}$ is bigger.

Which is bigger?

$\frac{1}{4}$ or $\frac{1}{3}$ $\boxed{\frac{1}{3}}$	$\frac{5}{6}$ or $\frac{7}{9}$ $\boxed{\frac{5}{6}}$	$\frac{1}{2}$ or $\frac{5}{8}$ $\boxed{\frac{5}{8}}$	$\frac{4}{9}$ or $\frac{1}{3}$ $\boxed{\frac{4}{9}}$
$\frac{2}{5}$ or $\frac{3}{8}$ $\boxed{\frac{2}{5}}$	$\frac{7}{10}$ or $\frac{8}{9}$ $\boxed{\frac{8}{9}}$	$\frac{8}{10}$ or $\frac{7}{8}$ $\boxed{\frac{7}{8}}$	$\frac{7}{12}$ or $\frac{2}{3}$ $\boxed{\frac{2}{3}}$
$\frac{2}{5}$ or $\frac{5}{8}$ $\boxed{\frac{2}{5}}$	$\frac{4}{15}$ or $\frac{1}{3}$ $\boxed{\frac{1}{3}}$	$\frac{3}{5}$ or $\frac{2}{3}$ $\boxed{\frac{2}{3}}$	$\frac{3}{8}$ or $\frac{1}{4}$ $\boxed{\frac{3}{8}}$

Which two fractions in each row are equal?

$\frac{1}{4}$	$\frac{3}{8}$	$\frac{4}{12}$	$\frac{3}{12}$	$\frac{7}{8}$	$\frac{5}{8}$	$\frac{1}{4}$ and $\frac{3}{12}$
$\frac{5}{8}$	$\frac{6}{9}$	$\frac{7}{10}$	$\frac{8}{12}$	$\frac{1}{2}$	$\frac{3}{4}$	$\frac{6}{9}$ and $\frac{8}{12}$
$\frac{7}{12}$	$\frac{6}{14}$	$\frac{7}{14}$	$\frac{3}{8}$	$\frac{4}{8}$	$\frac{9}{12}$	$\frac{7}{14}$ and $\frac{4}{8}$
$\frac{3}{8}$	$\frac{3}{9}$	$\frac{2}{6}$	$\frac{4}{7}$	$\frac{9}{10}$	$\frac{6}{7}$	$\frac{3}{9}$ and $\frac{2}{6}$
$\frac{3}{10}$	$\frac{5}{15}$	$\frac{2}{10}$	$\frac{3}{15}$	$\frac{4}{10}$	$\frac{7}{15}$	$\frac{2}{10}$ and $\frac{3}{15}$

Put these fractions in order starting with the smallest.

$\frac{1}{2}$	$\frac{5}{6}$	$\frac{2}{3}$	$\frac{1}{2}$	$\frac{2}{3}$	$\frac{5}{6}$
$\frac{5}{8}$	$\frac{3}{4}$	$\frac{11}{12}$	$\frac{5}{8}$	$\frac{3}{4}$	$\frac{11}{12}$
$\frac{2}{3}$	$\frac{8}{15}$	$\frac{3}{5}$	$\frac{8}{15}$	$\frac{3}{5}$	$\frac{2}{3}$

Difficulty in finding a common denominator indicates a weakness in times tables knowledge. Children need to convert all the fractions in the later questions into a common form before answering the question. Be careful that they do not try to guess the answer.

Converting fractions to decimals

Convert these fractions to decimals.

$\frac{3}{10}$ = $\boxed{0.3}$

(because the three goes in the tenths column)

$\frac{7}{100}$ = $\boxed{0.07}$

(because the seven goes in the hundredths column)

Convert these fractions to decimals.

$\frac{6}{10}$ = $\boxed{0.6}$	$\frac{9}{100}$ = $\boxed{0.09}$	$\frac{4}{100}$ = $\boxed{0.04}$	$\frac{6}{100}$ = $\boxed{0.06}$
$\frac{4}{10}$ = $\boxed{0.4}$	$\frac{2}{10}$ = $\boxed{0.4}$	$\frac{1}{10}$ = $\boxed{0.1}$	$\frac{7}{100}$ = $\boxed{0.07}$
$\frac{8}{100}$ = $\boxed{0.08}$	$\frac{5}{10}$ = $\boxed{0.5}$	$\frac{7}{10}$ = $\boxed{0.7}$	$\frac{8}{10}$ = $\boxed{0.8}$
$\frac{2}{100}$ = $\boxed{0.02}$	$\frac{5}{100}$ = $\boxed{0.05}$	$\frac{1}{100}$ = $\boxed{0.01}$	$\frac{3}{10}$ = $\boxed{0.3}$

Convert $\frac{1}{4}$ to a decimal.

To do this we have to divide the bottom number into the top.

When we run out of numbers we put in the decimal point and enough noughts to finish the sum. Be careful to keep the decimal point in your answer above the decimal point in the sum.

$$\begin{array}{r} 0.25 \\ 4\overline{)1.00} \end{array}$$

Convert these fractions to decimals.

$\frac{1}{2}$ = $\boxed{0.5}$	$\frac{3}{4}$ = $\boxed{0.75}$	$\frac{2}{5}$ = $\boxed{0.4}$	$\frac{1}{5}$ = $\boxed{0.2}$
$\frac{4}{5}$ = $\boxed{0.8}$	$\frac{3}{8}$ = $\boxed{0.375}$	$\frac{3}{5}$ = $\boxed{0.6}$	$\frac{1}{4}$ = $\boxed{0.25}$

Difficulty in the first section highlights weakness in understanding place value to the first two decimal places. It may be necessary to reinforce understanding of 10ths and 100ths in decimals.

Addition

Work out the answer to each sum.

```
    634              1 472
  4 812                 96
+ 1 428              8 391
  -----            +  564
  6 874             ------
                    10 523
```

Remember to carry if you need to.

Work out the answer to each sum.

5 831 8 375 + 219 **14 425**	3 724 9 942 + 623 **14 289**	9 994 7 358 + 471 **17 823**	524 7 034 + 95 **7 653**
7 341 299 + 5 143 **12 783**	9 328 347 + 8 222 **17 897**	7 159 39 + 748 **7 946**	208 4 943 + 55 **5 206**

Work out the answer to each sum.

8 594 629 9 878 + 96 **19 197**	7 362 843 4 732 + 53 **12 990**	3 041 571 5 210 + 71 **8 893**	7 641 93 8 521 + 843 **17 098**
8 795 659 3 212 + 961 **13 627**	6 043 4 147 + 8 948 **15 142**	27 153 8 612 + 127 **8 919**	146 3 714 26 + 5 003 **8 889**

This page should be fairly straightforward, but errors may creep in as the lists get longer towards the end. Errors will most likely be mistakes in adding the longer lists, adding across place value, or a failure to carry.

More addition

Work out the answer to each sum.

```
  23 714           11 541
   9 024              861
+    348           29 652
  ------           +    5
  33 086           ------
                   42 059
```

Remember to carry if you need to.

Work out the answer to each sum.

17 203 112 + 5 608 **22 923**	29 521 6 211 + 58 **35 790**	65 214 973 + 1 291 **67 478**	25 046 15 + 263 **25 324**
6 958 71 + 16 911 **23 940**	73 009 3 + 581 **73 593**	11 536 48 + 2 435 **14 019**	87 019 127 + 5 652 **92 798**

Work out the answer to each sum.

79 622 8 011 47 391 + 7 **135 031**	64 599 122 6 375 + 91 **71 187**	6 940 936 58 274 + 36 **66 186**	72 148 999 7 481 + 21 685 **102 313**
58 975 858 8 423 + 27 **68 283**	36 403 73 712 + 6 229 **43 417**	8 22 849 502 + 4 034 **27 393**	23 99 951 358 + 6 231 **106 563**

Any problems on this page will be similar to those encountered on the previous page. As the numbers get larger there is more opportunity for errors to occur.

Subtraction ⭐

Work out the answer to each sum.

```
  7 131            6 11
   843            4 721
 −  64           −  287
   779            4 434
```

Work out the answer to each sum.

```
  5 12 1          7 10 1          8 12 1          4 11 1
   635            937            937            528
 −  76          −  53          −  38          −  59
   559            759            899            469

  5 11 1          6 9 1           8 1             3 17 1
   628            705            297            483
 −  29          −  76          −  58          −  94
   599            629            239            389

  7 14 1          2 15 1          16 5 1          1 13 1
   854            362            963            248
 −  65          −  75          −  79          −  89
   789            287            884            159

  4 12 1          1 14 1          3 15 1          2 11 1
   537            238            461            322
 −  78          −  69          −  77          −  39
   459            189            384            283
```

Write the answer in the box.

317 − 49 = 268   286 − 98 = 188

423 − 85 = 338   176 − 87 = 89

Larry has 221 marbles. The lid comes off his tin and he loses 57. How many does he have left?

164 marbles

```
  1 11
  221
 −  57
  164
```

A school tuck shop has 537 packets of crisps. If they sell 69 packets how many are left?

468 packets

```
  4 12 1
   537
 −  69
   468
```

Children often take the smaller digit on the top away from the larger digit below. They should realise when sums require decomposition, or "stealing" from the digit on the left. In the second section, ensure that they are subtracting digits with the same place value.

More subtraction

Work out the answer to each sum.

```
  2 14 1          2 5 1
  3 154           2 561
 −  665          −   72
  2 489           2 289
```

Work out the answer to each sum.

```
  4 6 13 1        5 13 1           15 5 1          7 12 1
  3 743           5 642           5 642           8 235
 −  844          −  756          −  683          −  436
  4 899           5 585           4 959           7 799

  5 13 7 1        0 4 14 1         1 12 1          2 5 1
  6 484           1 257           2 354           2 368
 −  786          −  458          −  365          −  289
  5 698            799            1 989           2 079

  4 12 1          5 13 1          17 12 1          5 12 1
  5 323           3 641           2 833           6 321
 −  555          −  482          −  954          −  632
  4 768           3 159           1 879           5 689

  3 10 1
  7 412           8 236           5 423           6 13 1
 −  63          −  58          −  74            3 741
  7 349           8 178           5 349         −  82
                                                  3 659

  1 10 1          2 8 1
  5 213           7 391           4 822           1 6 5 1
 −  84          −  94          −  66            1 765
  5 129           7 297           4 756         −  87
                                                  1 678
```

At a pop concert 865 programmes are sold. If 2 345 people are at the concert how many do not have programmes?

1 480 people

```
  1 13 1
  2 345
 −  865
  1 480
```

A bakery makes 6 243 loaves. If 455 loaves are returned unsold, how many were sold?

5 788 loaves

```
  5 13 1
  6 243
 −  455
  5 788
```

The work on this page is similar to the previous page but involves larger amounts and wider differences between the numbers subtracted.

Subtraction with two zeros on top ⭐

Work out the answer to each sum.

```
  4 9 1           1 6 9 1
   500            2 700
 −  94          −  927
   406            1 773
```

Work out the answer to each sum.

```
  6 9 1           0 9 1           2 9 1           1 9 1
   700            100            300            200
 −  84          −  61          −  29          −  76
   616             39            271            124

  7 9 1           8 9 1           3 9 1           4 9 1
   800            900            400            500
 −  223          −  364          −  295          −  173
   577            536            105            327

  3 9 1           8 9 1           7 9 1           5 9 1
   400            900            800            600
 −  235          −  741          −  382          −  253
   165            159            418            347

  5 9 1           3 9 1           1 9 1           8 10 9 1
  7 600           6 400           5 200           9 100
 −  599          −  324          −  168          −  138
  7 001           6 076           5 032           8 962

  1 9 1           1 2 9 1          6 9 1           1 9 1
  8 200           3 400           6 300           8 100
 −  323          −  749          −  416          −  591
  7 877           4 651           5 884           7 509

  6 1 4 9 1       1 2 9 1         7 2 9 1          1 2 9 1
  7 500           9 300           8 200           5 300
 −  562          −  359          −  274          −  833
  6 938           8 941           7 926           4 467

  5 1 3 9 1       3 1 9 1          6 9 1           5 1 5 9 1
  6 400           9 200           4 700           6 600
 −  749          −  362          −  643          −  821
  5 651           8 838           4 057           5 779
```

The number on the top has two noughts in the tens and units columns. Children will need first to bring one digit from the hundreds column to the tens column (to make ten tens), and then take one of the tens to the units column. Then do the sum in the usual way.

Real life problems

A ship sails 526 km to port A and then 753 km to port B. What is the total distance travelled?

1 279 kilometres

```
   526
 + 753
  1 279
```

In a sponsored walk, Sam and Karen walked a combined distance of 19 642 metres. If Karen walked 9 476 metres how far did Sam walk?

10 166 metres

```
  5 13 1
  19 642
 − 9 476
  10 166
```

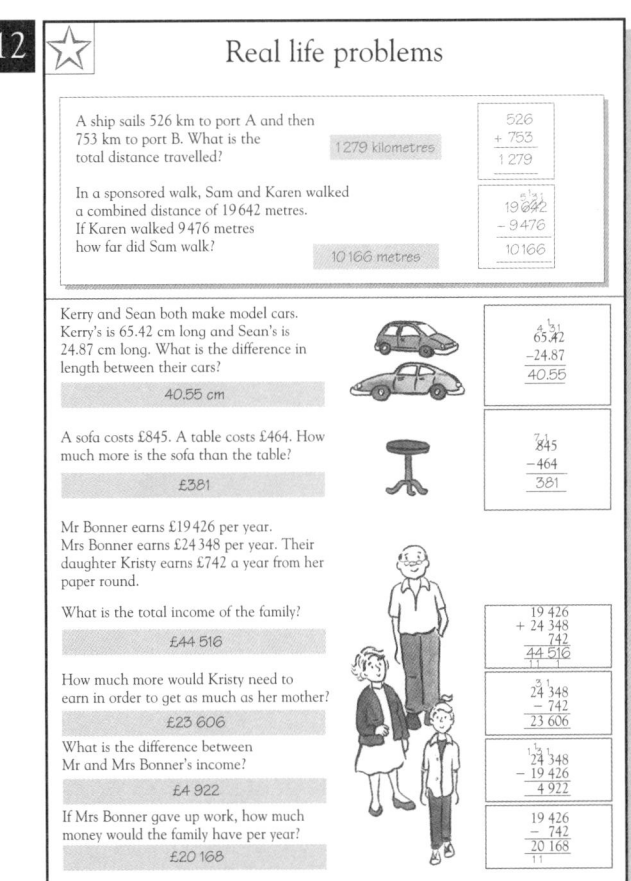

Kerry and Sean both make model cars. Kerry's is 65.42 cm long and Sean's is 24.87 cm long. What is the difference in length between their cars?

40.55 cm

```
  4 13 1
  65.42
 −24.87
  40.55
```

A sofa costs £845. A table costs £464. How much more is the sofa than the table?

£381

```
  7 14 1
  845
 −464
  381
```

Mr Bonner earns £19 426 per year. Mrs Bonner earns £24 348 per year. Their daughter Kristy earns £742 a year from her paper round.

What is the total income of the family?

£44 516

```
  19 426
 + 24 348
    742
  44 516
  1 1
```

How much more would Kristy need to earn in order to get as much as her mother?

£23 606

```
  3 1
  24 348
 −   742
  23 606
```

What is the difference between Mr and Mrs Bonner's income?

£4 922

```
  1 1
  24 348
 − 19 426
   4 922
```

If Mrs Bonner gave up work, how much money would the family have per year?

£20 168

```
  19 426
 −   742
  20 168
  1 1
```

On this page and the following two, children can revise their skills of addition and subtraction with real life problems. If they are unsure which operation to use, discuss whether the answer will be larger (addition) or smaller (subtraction).

Real life problems

A plumber has 6 m of copper tubing. If he uses 2.36 m, how much will he have left?

3.64 m

```
  5  9
  6.00
− 2.36
  3.64
```

If he buys another 4.5 m of copper tubing, how much will he now have?

8.14 m

```
  3.64
+ 4.50
  8.14
    1
```

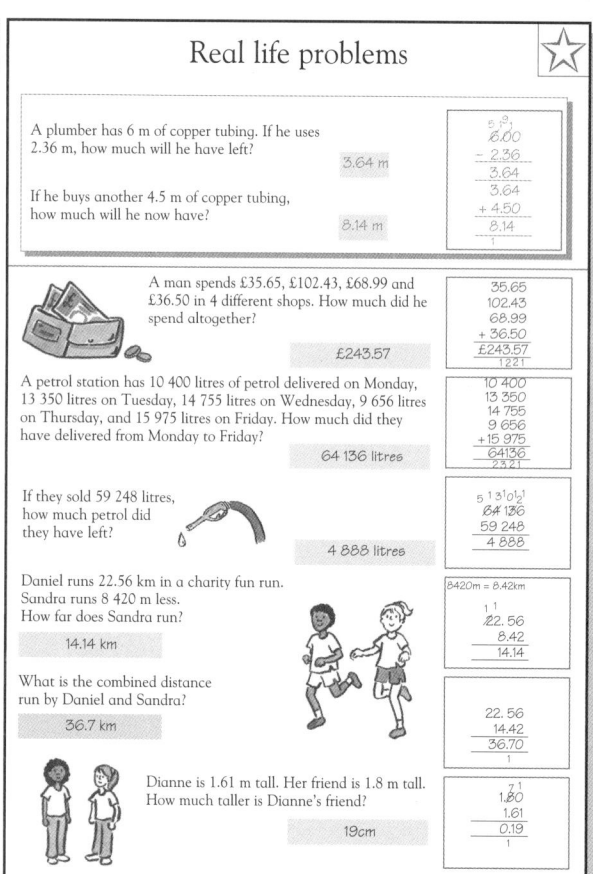

A man spends £35.65, £102.43, £68.99 and £36.50 in 4 different shops. How much did he spend altogether?

£243.57

```
   35.65
  102.43
   68.99
 + 36.50
 £243.57
    1221
```

A petrol station has 10 400 litres of petrol delivered on Monday, 13 350 litres on Tuesday, 14 755 litres on Wednesday, 9 656 litres on Thursday, and 15 975 litres on Friday. How much did they have delivered from Monday to Friday?

64 136 litres

```
  10 400
  13 350
  14 755
   9 656
 +15 975
  64136
   2321
```

If they sold 59 248 litres, how much petrol did they have left?

4 888 litres

```
  5 13 10 1
  64 136
  59 248
   4 888
```

Daniel runs 22.56 km in a charity fun run. Sandra runs 8 420 m less. How far does Sandra run?

14.14 km

```
8420m = 8.42km
  1 1
  22.56
   8.42
  14.14
```

What is the combined distance run by Daniel and Sandra?

36.7 km

```
  22.56
  14.42
  36.70
```

Dianne is 1.61 m tall. Her friend is 1.8 m tall. How much taller is Dianne's friend?

19cm

```
   7 1
  1.80
  1.61
  0.19
    1
```

This page also helps children revise their skills of addition and subtraction in real life situations. Take care when units of measurement need to be converted.

Real life problems

A man walks 18.34 km on Saturday and 16.57 km on Sunday. How far did he walk that weekend?

34.91 km

```
  18.34
 +16.57
  34.91
   1 1
```

How much further did he walk on Saturday?

1.77 km

```
   7 7 1
  18.34
 −16.57
   1.77
```

A rectangular field measures 103.7 m by 96.5 m. How long is the perimeter of the field?

400.4 m

```
  103.7      207.4
 ×   2     +193.0
  207.4      400.4
           96.5
         ×   2
         193.0
```

When Joe and Kerry stand on a weighing machine it reads 136.53 kg. When Joe steps off, it reads 68.76 kg. How much does Joe weigh?

67.77kg

```
  0 12 15 14
  136.53
 − 68.76
   67.77
```

A rectangular room has an area of 32.58 m². When a carpet is put down there is still 7.99 m² of floor showing. What is the area of the carpet?

24.59 m²

```
  2 11 14 1
  32.58
 −  7.99
  24.59
```

A brother and sister's combined height is 3.27 m. If the sister is 1.59 m tall, how tall is the brother?

1.68 m

```
  2 11 1
  3.27
 − 1.59
  1.68
```

A country has 4 motorways, the MA which is 1 246 km long, the MB which is 339 km long, the MC which is 1 573 km long, and the MD is 48 km long. How much motorway does the country have in total?

3 206 Km

```
  1 246
    339
  1 573
 +   48
  3206
   1 22
```

Jenny's aquarium holds 25.56 litres of water. She buys a new one which holds 32 litres. How much extra water do her fish have?

6.44 litres

```
  2 1 9 1
  32.00
 −25.56
   6.44
```

This page once again helps children revise their skills of addition and subtraction in real life situations. In the first question, ensure that they are finding the perimeter and not the area.

Simple use of brackets

Work out these sums.

(4 + 6) − (2 + 1) = 10 − 3 = 7

(2 x 5) + (10 − 4) = 10 + 6 = 16

Remember to work out the brackets first.

Work out these sums.

(5 + 3) + (6 − 2) = 12   (3 − 1) + (12 − 1) = 13

(6 − 1) − (1 + 2) = 2   (9 + 5) − (3 + 6) = 5

(8 + 3) + (12 − 2) = 21   (14 + 12) − (9 + 4) = 13

(7 − 2) + (4 + 5) = 14   (9 − 3) − (4 + 2) = 0

Now try these longer sums.

(5 + 9) + (12 − 2) − (4 + 3) = 17

(10 + 5) − (2 + 4) + (9 + 6) = 24

(19 + 4) − (3 + 2) − (2 + 1) = 15

(24 − 5) − (3 + 7) − (5 − 2) = 6

(15 + 3) + (7 − 2) − (5 + 7) = 11

Now try these. Be careful, the brackets now have multiplication sums.

(2 x 3) + (5 x 2) = 16   (3 x 4) − (2 x 2) = 8

(7 x 2) + (3 x 3) = 23   (5 x 4) − (3 x 2) = 14

(6 x 4) − (4 x 3) = 12   (9 x 5) − (4 x 6) = 21

(12 x 4) − (8 x 3) = 24   (7 x 4) − (8 x 2) = 12

If the answer is 24, which of these sums gives the correct answer? Write the letter in the box.

a (3 + 5) + (3 x 1)   c (3 x 5) + (3 x 3)   e (5 x 7) − (2 x 5)
b (3 x 5) + (3 x 2)   d (2 x 5) + (2 x 6)   f (6 + 7) + (12 − 2)

(c)

Errors on this page will most likely be the result of choosing the wrong order of operation. Remind children that they must work out the brackets first, before they add or subtract the results. Concentration and careful reading should prevent any problems.

Simple use of brackets

Work out these sums.

(3 + 2) x (4 + 1) = 5 x 5 = 25

(10 x 5) ÷ (10 − 5) = 50 ÷ 5 = 10

Remember to work out the brackets first.

Work out these sums.

(7 + 3) x (8 − 4) = 40   (5 − 2) x (8 − 1) = 21

(9 + 5) ÷ (1 + 6) = 2   (14 − 6) x (4 + 3) = 56

(14 + 4) ÷ (12 − 6) = 3   (9 + 21) ÷ (8 − 5) = 10

(11 − 5) x (7 + 5) = 72   (8 + 20) ÷ (12 − 10) = 14

(6 + 9) ÷ (8 − 3) = 3   (14 − 3) x (6 + 1) = 77

(10 + 10) ÷ (2 + 3) = 4   (9 + 3) x (2 + 4) = 72

Now try these.

(4 x 3) ÷ (1 x 2) = 6   (5 x 4) ÷ (2 x 2) = 5

(8 x 5) ÷ (4 x 1) = 10   (6 x 4) ÷ (3 x 4) = 2

(2 x 4) x (2 x 3) = 48   (3 x 5) x (1 x 2) = 30

(8 x 4) ÷ (2 x 2) = 8   (6 x 4) ÷ (4 x 2) = 3

If the answer is 30, which of these sums gives the correct answer?

a (3 x 5) x (2 x 2)   d (20 ÷ 2) x (12 ÷ 3)
b (4 x 5) x (5 x 2)   e (5 x 12) ÷ (2 x 5)
c (12 x 5) ÷ (8 ÷ 4)   f (9 x 5) ÷ (10 ÷ 2)

c

If the answer is 8, which of these sums gives the correct answer?

a (16 ÷ 2) ÷ (2 x 1)   d (24 ÷ 6) x (8 ÷ 4)
b (9 ÷ 3) x (3 x 2)   e (8 ÷ 4) x (8 ÷ 1)
c (12 x 4) ÷ (6 x 2)   f (16 ÷ 4) x (20 ÷ 4)

d

This page continues the work of the previous page, but the brackets are multiplied or divided. It may be necessary to remind children to read carefully, as several operations take place in each sum.

17 — Simple use of brackets

Work out these sums.
$(5 + 3) + (9 − 2) = \boxed{8 + 7 = 15}$
$(5 + 2) − (4 − 1) = \boxed{7 − 3 = 4}$
$(4 + 2) \times (3 + 1) = \boxed{6 \times 4 = 24}$
$(3 \times 5) \div (9 − 6) = \boxed{15 \div 3 = 5}$
Remember to work out the brackets first.

Work out these sums.

$(5 + 4) + (7 − 3) =$	13	$(9 − 2) + (6 + 4) =$	17
$(7 + 3) − (9 − 7) =$	8	$(15 − 5) + (2 + 3) =$	15
$(11 \times 2) − (3 \times 2) =$	16	$(15 \div 3) + (9 \times 2) =$	23
$(12 \times 2) − (3 \times 3) =$	15	$(6 \div 2) + (8 \times 2) =$	19
$(9 \times 3) − (7 \times 3) =$	6	$(15 \div 5) + (3 \times 4) =$	15
$(20 \div 5) − (8 \div 2) =$	0	$(5 \times 10) − (12 \times 4) =$	2

Now try these.

$(4 + 8) \div (3 \times 2) =$	2	$(6 \times 4) \div (3 \times 2) =$	4
$(9 + 5) \div (2 \times 1) =$	7	$(7 \times 4) \div (3 + 4) =$	4
$(3 + 6) \times (3 \times 3) =$	81	$(5 \times 5) \div (10 \div 2) =$	5
$(24 \div 2) \times (3 \times 2) =$	72	$(8 \times 6) \div (2 \times 12) =$	2

Write down the letters of all the sums that make 25.
a $(2 \times 5) \times (3 \times 2)$ d $(40 \div 2) + (10 \div 2)$
b $(5 \times 5) + (7 − 2)$ e $(10 \times 5) − (5 \times 5)$
c $(6 \times 5) − (10 \div 2)$ f $(10 \times 10) \div (10 − 6)$

c, d, e, f

Write down the letters of all the sums that make 20.
a $(10 \div 2) \times (4 \div 4)$ d $(20 \div 4) \times (8 + 2)$
b $(7 \times 3) − (3 \div 3)$ e $(10 \div 2) + (20 \div 2)$
c $(8 \times 4) − (6 \times 2)$ f $(14 \div 2) + (2 \times 7)$

b, c

This page reinforces all the elements of the previous two pages. Again, the most likely cause of error will be lack of concentration.

18 — Multiplying decimals

Work out these sums.

4.6	3.9	8.4
x 3	x 5	x 8
13.8	19.5	67.2
1	4	3

Work out these sums.

4.7	9.1	5.8	1.7	5.1
x 3	x 3	x 3	x 2	x 2
14.1	27.3	17.4	3.4	10.2

7.4	3.6	6.5	4.2	3.8
x 2	x 4	x 4	x 2	x 2
14.8	14.4	26.0	8.4	7.6

4.2	4.7	1.8	3.4	3.7
x 4	x 4	x 5	x 5	x 5
16.8	18.8	9.0	17.0	18.5

2.5	2.4	5.3	7.2	5.1
x 5	x 6	x 7	x 8	x 9
12.5	14.4	37.1	57.6	45.9

7.9	8.6	8.8	7.5	9.9
x 9	x 9	x 8	x 8	x 6
71.1	77.4	70.4	60.0	59.4

6.8	5.7	6.9	7.5	8.4
x 7	x 6	x 7	x 9	x 9
47.6	34.2	48.3	67.5	75.6

7.3	2.8	3.8	7.7	9.4
x 8	x 7	x 8	x 7	x 9
58.4	19.6	30.4	53.9	84.6

Ensure that children work from right to left. Problems will highlight gaps in their knowledge of times tables. Remind them that the number they are multiplying has one decimal place, so their answer must have one decimal place also, and this can be put in at the end.

19 — Multiplying decimals

Work out these sums.

37.5	26.2	65.3
x 2	x 5	x 9
75.0	131.0	587.7
1 1	3 1	4 2

Work out these sums.

53.3	93.2	51.4	34.6	35.2
x 2	x 2	x 2	x 3	x 3
106.6	186.4	102.8	103.8	105.6

46.5	25.8	16.4	47.1	37.4
x 4	x 4	x 3	x 5	x 5
186.0	103.2	49.2	235.5	187.0

12.4	46.3	17.5	36.5	72.4
x 5	x 5	x 6	x 6	x 7
62.0	231.5	105.0	219.0	506.8

37.5	20.3	73.4	92.6	47.9
x 7	x 7	x 7	x 6	x 6
262.5	142.1	513.8	555.6	287.4

53.9	75.6	28.8	79.4	99.9
x 8	x 8	x 8	x 8	x 9
431.2	604.8	230.4	635.2	899.1

37.9	14.8	35.4	46.8	27.2
x 9	x 9	x 9	x 8	x 7
341.1	133.2	318.6	374.4	190.4

39.5	84.2	68.5	73.2	47.6
x 6	x 9	x 8	x 9	x 6
237.0	757.8	548.0	658.8	285.6

This page further revises decimal multiplication, using larger numbers.

20 — Real life problems

Nigel earns £1.50 a day on his paper round. How much does he earn per week?

£10.50

£1.50
x 7
£10.50
3

When Ivan subtracts the width of his cupboard from the length of his bedroom wall he finds he has 3.65 m of wall space left. If the cupboard is 0.87m wide, what is the length of his bedroom wall?

4.52 m

3.65 m
+0.87 m
4.52 m
1 1

Sophie buys her mother a bunch of flowers for £12.95 and her brothers some sweets for £2.76. If she has £7.83 left how much did she start with?

£23.54

12.95	15.71
+ 2.76	+ 7.83
15.71	23.54
1 1	1 1

If David were 7.5 cm taller, he would be twice as tall as Ian. Ian is 74.25 cm tall, so how tall is David?

141 cm (1.41 m)

74.25	148.5
x 2	− 7.5
148.50	141.0
1	

Stanley is making some shelves which are 75.5 cm long. If the wood he is using is 180 cm long, how many pieces will he need to make six shelves?

3 pieces

2 shelves per piece with some wastage
6 ÷ 2 = 3

A café uses 27.5 litres of milk a day. If they have a weekly delivery of 180 litres, how much will they have left after six days?

15 litres

27.5	7 1 180
x 6	− 165
165.0	15
4 3	

Charles has 12.5 m of railway track. Gavin has 8.6 m and Kristy has 4.8 m. If they put their track together how long will their circuit be?

25.9 m

12.5
+ 8.6
4.8
25.9
1 1

This page provides an opportunity to apply the skills practised to real life problems. Children will need to choose the operation carefully. Some questions require more than one operation.

Real life problems

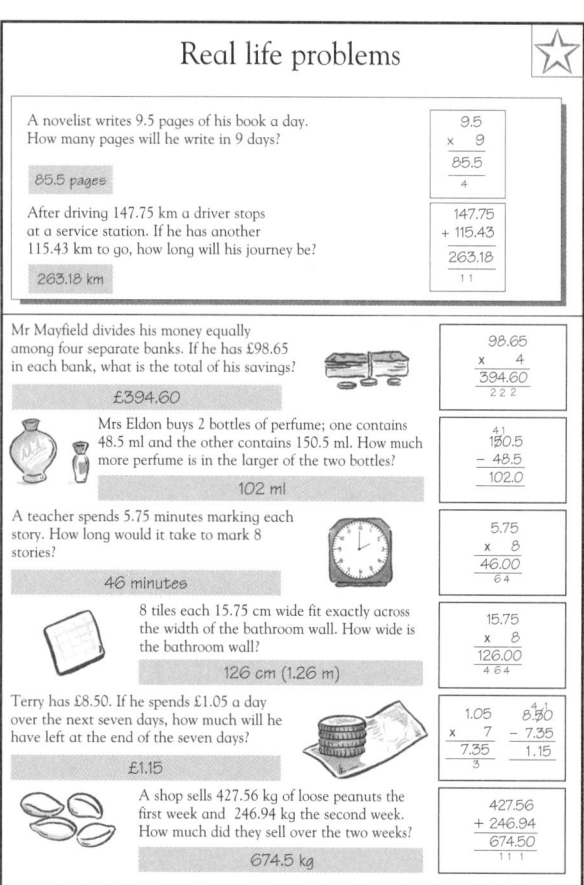

A novelist writes 9.5 pages of his book a day. How many pages will he write in 9 days?

85.5 pages

```
  9.5
x   9
 85.5
    4
```

After driving 147.75 km a driver stops at a service station. If he has another 115.43 km to go, how long will his journey be?

263.18 km

```
 147.75
+115.43
 263.18
    1 1
```

Mr Mayfield divides his money equally among four separate banks. If he has £98.65 in each bank, what is the total of his savings?

£394.60

```
 98.65
x    4
394.60
  2 2 2
```

Mrs Eldon buys 2 bottles of perfume; one contains 48.5 ml and the other contains 150.5 ml. How much more perfume is in the larger of the two bottles?

102 ml

```
  4 1
150.5
- 48.5
102.0
```

A teacher spends 5.75 minutes marking each story. How long would it take to mark 8 stories?

46 minutes

```
  5.75
x    8
46.00
  6 4
```

8 tiles each 15.75 cm wide fit exactly across the width of the bathroom wall. How wide is the bathroom wall?

126 cm (1.26 m)

```
 15.75
x    8
126.00
  4 6 4
```

Terry has £8.50. If he spends £1.05 a day over the next seven days, how much will he have left at the end of the seven days?

£1.15

```
 1.05      8.50
x   7    - 7.35
 7.35      1.15
   3
```

A shop sells 427.56 kg of loose peanuts the first week and 246.94 kg the second week. How much did they sell over the two weeks?

674.5 kg

```
 427.56
+246.94
 674.50
   1 1 1
```

Another page that revises various operations in real life situations.

Real life problems

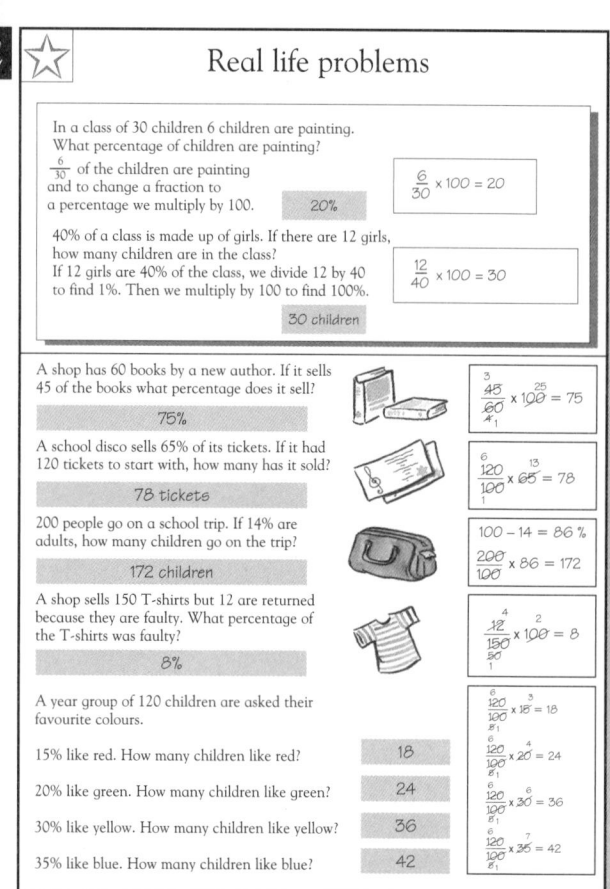

In a class of 30 children 6 children are painting. What percentage of children are painting? $\frac{6}{30}$ of the children are painting and to change a fraction to a percentage we multiply by 100.

20%

$$\frac{6}{30} \times 100 = 20$$

40% of a class is made up of girls. If there are 12 girls, how many children are in the class? If 12 girls are 40% of the class, we divide 12 by 40 to find 1%. Then we multiply by 100 to find 100%.

30 children

$$\frac{12}{40} \times 100 = 30$$

A shop has 60 books by a new author. If it sells 45 of the books what percentage does it sell?

75%

$$\frac{\overset{3}{45}}{\underset{4}{60}} \times \overset{25}{100} = 75$$

A school disco sells 65% of its tickets. If it had 120 tickets to start with, how many has it sold?

78 tickets

$$\frac{\overset{6}{120}}{100} \times \overset{13}{65} = 78$$

200 people go on a school trip. If 14% are adults, how many children go on the trip?

172 children

$$100 - 14 = 86\%$$
$$\frac{200}{100} \times 86 = 172$$

A shop sells 150 T-shirts but 12 are returned because they are faulty. What percentage of the T-shirts was faulty?

8%

$$\frac{\overset{4}{12}}{\underset{1}{150}} \times \overset{2}{100} = 8$$

A year group of 120 children are asked their favourite colours.

15% like red. How many children like red?   18

20% like green. How many children like green?   24

30% like yellow. How many children like yellow?   36

35% like blue. How many children like blue?   42

$$\frac{\overset{6}{120}}{100} \times \overset{3}{15} = 18$$
$$\frac{\overset{6}{120}}{100} \times \overset{5}{20} = 24$$
$$\frac{\overset{6}{120}}{100} \times \overset{6}{30} = 36$$
$$\frac{\overset{6}{120}}{100} \times \overset{7}{35} = 42$$

In questions 1 and 4 children should see that the answer can be expressed as a fraction, which can then be converted to a percentage by multiplying by 100.

Real life problems

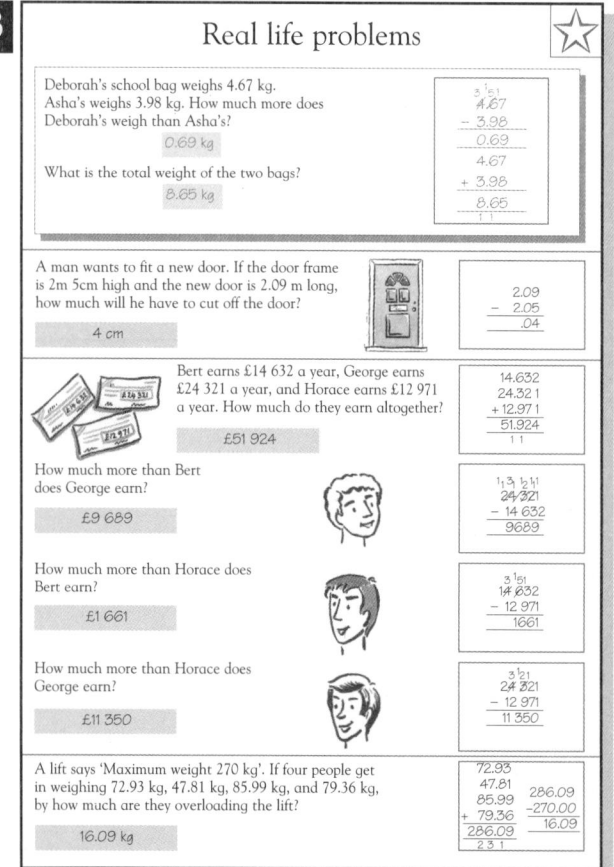

Deborah's school bag weighs 4.67 kg. Asha's weighs 3.98 kg. How much more does Deborah's weigh than Asha's?

0.69 kg

```
 3 1 6 1
  4.67
- 3.98
  0.69
```

What is the total weight of the two bags?

8.65 kg

```
  4.67
+ 3.98
  8.65
   1 1
```

A man wants to fit a new door. If the door frame is 2m 5cm high and the new door is 2.09 m long, how much will he have to cut off the door?

4 cm

```
 2.09
-2.05
  .04
```

Bert earns £14 632 a year, George earns £24 321 a year, and Horace earns £12 971 a year. How much do they earn altogether?

£51 924

```
 14.632
 24.321
+12.971
 51.924
    1 1
```

How much more than Bert does George earn?

£9 689

```
 1 3 1 3 1
 24 321
-14 632
  9 689
```

How much more than Horace does Bert earn?

£1 661

```
   3 1 5 1
 14 632
-12 971
  1 661
```

How much more than Horace does George earn?

£11 350

```
   3 1 2 1
 24 321
-12 971
 11 350
```

A lift says 'Maximum weight 270 kg'. If four people get in weighing 72.93 kg, 47.81 kg, 85.99 kg, and 79.36 kg, by how much are they overloading the lift?

16.09 kg

```
 72.93
 47.81
 85.99        286.09
+79.36      -270.00
286.09        16.09
  2 3 1
```

In the first question, it will be necessary to express both measurements in the same way, i.e. 2 m 5 cm is 2.05 m, or 2.09 m is 2 m 9 cm.

Comparing units

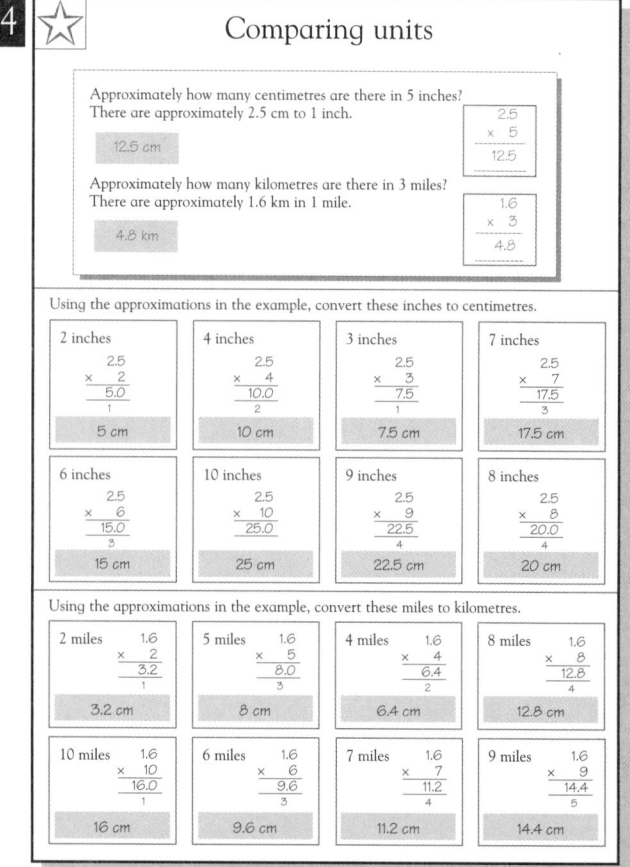

Approximately how many centimetres are there in 5 inches? There are approximately 2.5 cm to 1 inch.

12.5 cm

```
  2.5
x   5
 12.5
```

Approximately how many kilometres are there in 3 miles? There are approximately 1.6 km in 1 mile.

4.8 km

```
  1.6
x   3
  4.8
```

Using the approximations in the example, convert these inches to centimetres.

2 inches	4 inches	3 inches	7 inches
2.5 × 2 = 5.0	2.5 × 4 = 10.0	2.5 × 3 = 7.5	2.5 × 7 = 17.5
5 cm	10 cm	7.5 cm	17.5 cm

6 inches	10 inches	9 inches	8 inches
2.5 × 6 = 15.0	2.5 × 10 = 25.0	2.5 × 9 = 22.5	2.5 × 8 = 20.0
15 cm	25 cm	22.5 cm	20 cm

Using the approximations in the example, convert these miles to kilometres.

2 miles	5 miles	4 miles	8 miles
1.6 × 2 = 3.2	1.6 × 5 = 8.0	1.6 × 4 = 6.4	1.6 × 8 = 12.8
3.2 cm	8 cm	6.4 cm	12.8 cm

10 miles	6 miles	7 miles	9 miles
1.6 × 10 = 16.0	1.6 × 6 = 9.6	1.6 × 7 = 11.2	1.6 × 9 = 14.4
16 cm	9.6 cm	11.2 cm	14.4 cm

This page and the next should be fairly straightforward as children are given the conversion factors. Notice that they are required to multiply decimals, which has been practised earlier in this book. It is worth pointing out that these conversions are approximate.

Comparing units

Approximately how many pounds are there in 4 kg?
There are approximately 2.2 lb to 1 kg.

8.8 lb

$$\begin{array}{r} 2.2 \\ \times\ \ 4 \\ \hline 8.8 \end{array}$$

Approximately how many litres are there in 5 pints?
A pint is approximately 0.6 of a litre.

3.0 litres

$$\begin{array}{r} 0.6 \\ \times\ \ 5 \\ \hline 3.0 \end{array}$$

Using the approximations in the example, convert these kilograms to pounds.

2 kg	6 kg	3 kg	7 kg
$\begin{array}{r}2.2\\ \times\ 2\\ \hline 4.4\end{array}$	$\begin{array}{r}2.2\\ \times\ 6\\ \hline 13.2\end{array}$	$\begin{array}{r}2.2\\ \times\ 3\\ \hline 6.6\end{array}$	$\begin{array}{r}2.2\\ \times\ 7\\ \hline 15.4\end{array}$
4.4 lb	13.2 lb	6.6 lb	15.4 lb

5 kg	9 kg	8 kg	10 kg
$\begin{array}{r}2.2\\ \times\ 5\\ \hline 11.0\end{array}$	$\begin{array}{r}2.2\\ \times\ 9\\ \hline 19.8\end{array}$	$\begin{array}{r}2.2\\ \times\ 8\\ \hline 17.6\end{array}$	$\begin{array}{r}2.2\\ \times\ 10\\ \hline 22.0\end{array}$
11 lb	19.8 lb	17.6 lb	22 lb

Using the approximations in the example, convert these pints to litres.

10 pints	8 pints	2 pints	4 pints
$\begin{array}{r}0.6\\ \times\ 10\\ \hline 6.0\end{array}$	$\begin{array}{r}0.6\\ \times\ 8\\ \hline 4.8\end{array}$	$\begin{array}{r}0.6\\ \times\ 2\\ \hline 1.2\end{array}$	$\begin{array}{r}0.6\\ \times\ 4\\ \hline 2.4\end{array}$
6 litres	4.8 litres	1.2 litres	2.4 litres

7 pints	9 pints	3 pints	6 pints
$\begin{array}{r}0.6\\ \times\ 7\\ \hline 4.2\end{array}$	$\begin{array}{r}0.6\\ \times\ 9\\ \hline 5.4\end{array}$	$\begin{array}{r}0.6\\ \times\ 3\\ \hline 1.8\end{array}$	$\begin{array}{r}0.6\\ \times\ 6\\ \hline 3.6\end{array}$
4.2 litres	5.4 litres	1.8 litres	3.6 litres

Once again children are required to multiply decimals, which has been practised earlier in this book. Again, it is worth pointing out that these conversions are approximate.

Naming parts of a circle

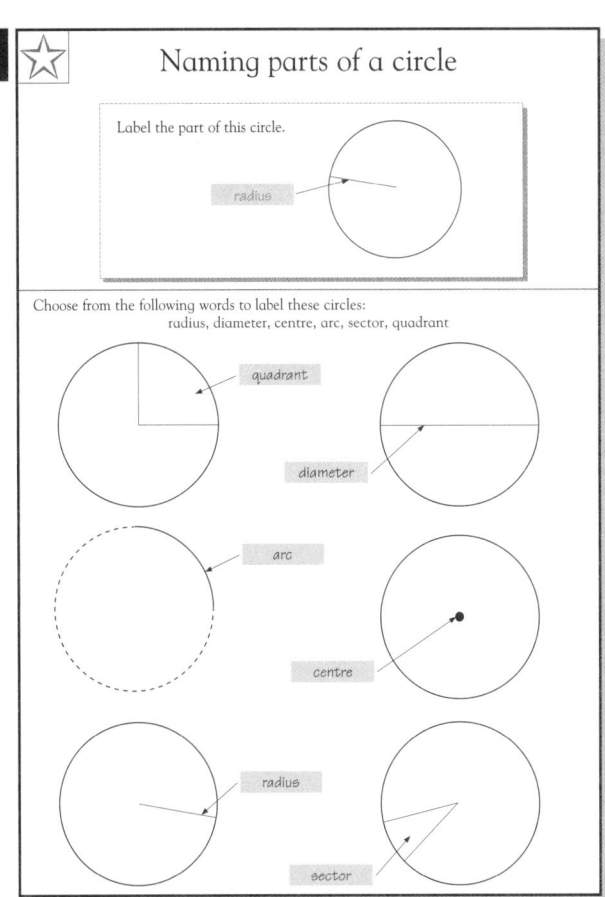

Label the part of this circle.

radius

Choose from the following words to label these circles:
radius, diameter, centre, arc, sector, quadrant

quadrant

diameter

arc

centre

radius

sector

This page requires children to label parts of a circle. As this page is knowledge-based, any mistakes should be discussed and the page should be revisited at a later date to check that the information has been retained.

Area of right-angled triangles

Find the area of this right-angled triangle.

Because the area of this triangle is half the area of the rectangle shown, we can find the area of the rectangle and then divide it by two to find the area of the triangle.
So the area = (8 cm x 4 cm) ÷ 2
= 32 ÷ 2 = 16 cm²

Area = 16 cm²

Find the area of these right-angled triangles.

5 cm, 3 cm, 12 cm → 30 cm²

10 cm → 15 cm²

9 cm, 2 cm → 9 cm²

4 cm, 14 cm → 28 cm²

5 cm, 6 cm → 15 cm²

6 cm, 8 cm → 24 cm²

12 cm, 6 cm → 36 cm²

20 cm → 30 cm²

3 cm, 7 cm, 4 cm → 14 cm²

The operation of multiplying the sides together and dividing by two should offer no serious difficulty to children, but make sure that they are really clear about why they are doing this.

Speed problems

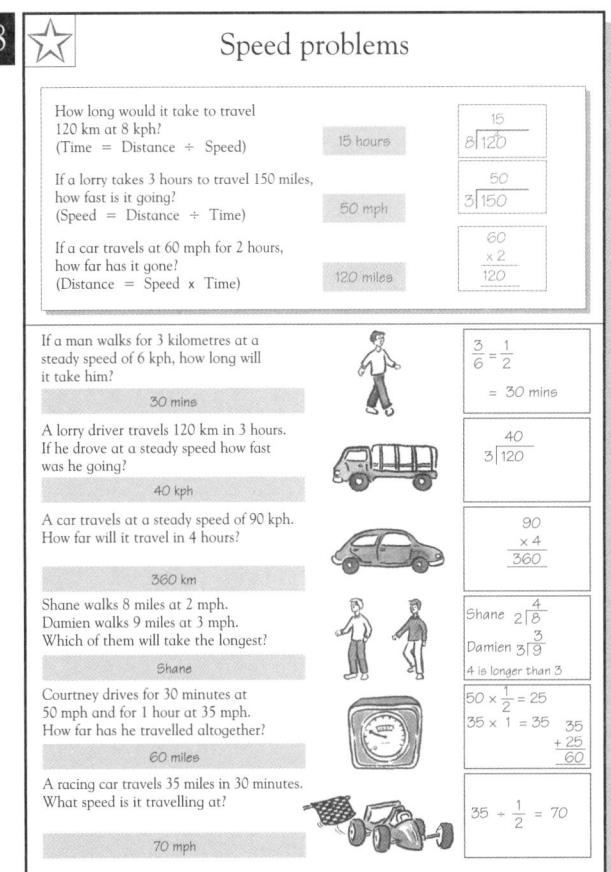

How long would it take to travel 120 km at 8 kph?
(Time = Distance ÷ Speed)

15 hours

$$8\overline{)120} = 15$$

If a lorry takes 3 hours to travel 150 miles, how fast is it going?
(Speed = Distance ÷ Time)

50 mph

$$3\overline{)150} = 50$$

If a car travels at 60 mph for 2 hours, how far has it gone?
(Distance = Speed x Time)

120 miles

$$\begin{array}{r}60\\ \times\ 2\\ \hline 120\end{array}$$

If a man walks for 3 kilometres at a steady speed of 6 kph, how long will it take him?

30 mins

$$\frac{3}{6} = \frac{1}{2}$$
$$= 30\ \text{mins}$$

A lorry driver travels 120 km in 3 hours. If he drove at a steady speed how fast was he going?

40 kph

$$3\overline{)120} = 40$$

A car travels at a steady speed of 90 kph. How far will it travel in 4 hours?

360 km

$$\begin{array}{r}90\\ \times\ 4\\ \hline 360\end{array}$$

Shane walks 8 miles at 2 mph. Damien walks 9 miles at 3 mph. Which of them will take the longest?

Shane

Shane $2\overline{)8} = 4$
Damien $3\overline{)9} = 3$
4 is longer than 3

Courtney drives for 30 minutes at 50 mph and for 1 hour at 35 mph. How far has he travelled altogether?

60 miles

$50 \times \frac{1}{2} = 25$
$35 \times 1 = 35$

$$\begin{array}{r}35\\ +\ 25\\ \hline 60\end{array}$$

A racing car travels 35 miles in 30 minutes. What speed is it travelling at?

70 mph

$$35 \div \frac{1}{2} = 70$$

If children experience difficulty on this page, ask them what they need to find, speed, distance or time, and refer them to the necessary formula. Encourage them to develop simple examples which will help them to remember the formulae.

Likely outcomes ☆

Throw a coin 20 times.
Keep a tally.

H	ꟾꟾꟾꟾ ꟾꟾꟾꟾ
T	ꟾꟾꟾꟾ ꟾꟾꟾꟾ ꟾ

Put your results on a bar chart.

Number of throws

What do you notice?

Heads and tails come up roughly the same number of times because there are only two possible outcomes, and they are equally likely.

Predict what you think the outcome would be if you tossed two coins 48 times.

2 heads 12 times   2 tails 12 times   1 of each 24 times

Now throw two coins 48 times yourself and record your results on this tally chart.

2 Heads	ꟾꟾꟾꟾ ꟾꟾꟾꟾ ꟾꟾꟾꟾ
2 Tails	ꟾꟾꟾꟾ ꟾꟾꟾꟾ ꟾꟾ
1 of each	ꟾꟾꟾꟾ ꟾꟾꟾꟾ ꟾꟾꟾꟾ ꟾꟾꟾꟾ ꟾ

Draw a bar chart to show your results.

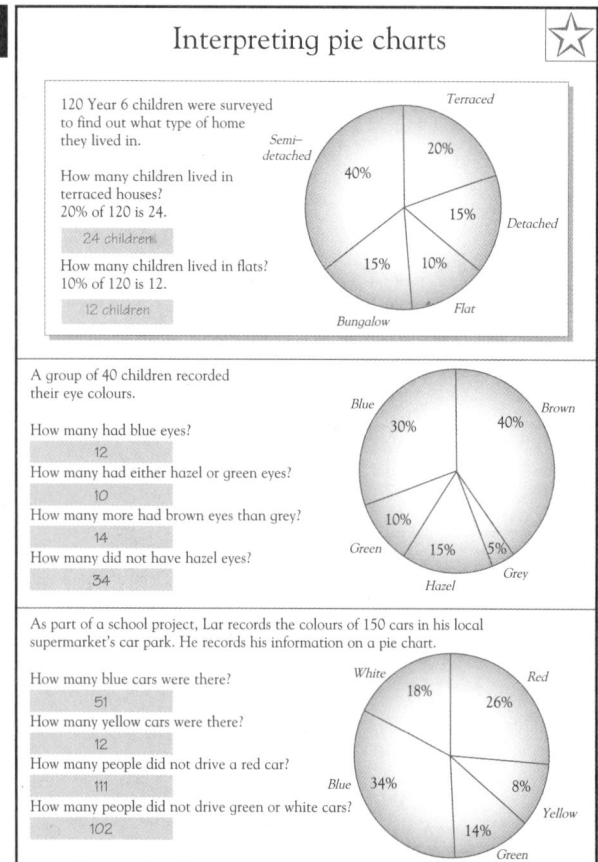

Number of throws

Heads   Tails   1 of each

Which result comes up the most often?   one of each

Can you explain why some results are more probable than others?

The child's answer should explain that there are four possible outcomes and that one of each has a two-in-four chance of coming up.

The child's prediction in the first question may be considerably different from the result. Once the work is done, check that the child can use the experience to improve his or her understanding of likely outcomes. The tally chart may differ from the one shown here.

Interpreting pie charts

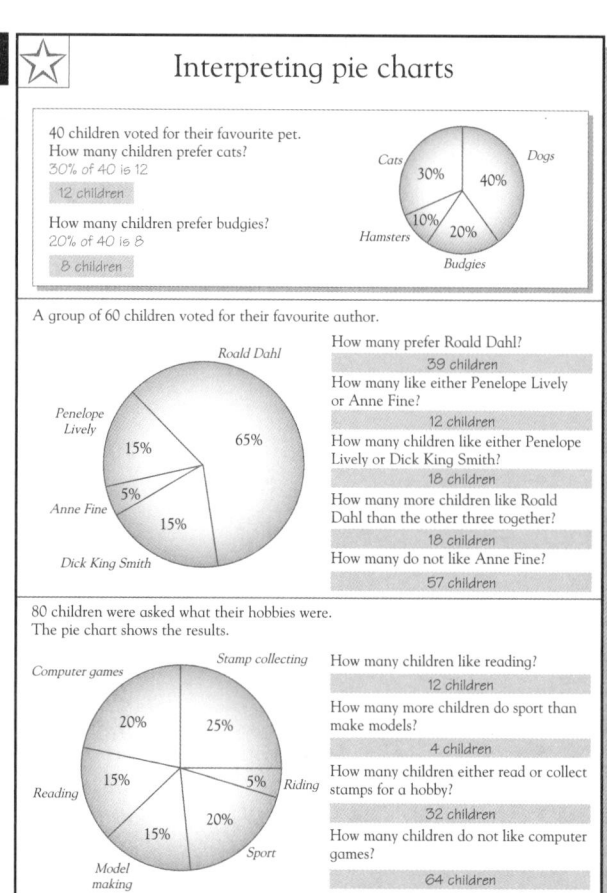

40 children voted for their favourite pet.
How many children prefer cats?
30% of 40 is 12
12 children

How many children prefer budgies?
20% of 40 is 8
8 children

A group of 60 children voted for their favourite author.

How many prefer Roald Dahl?
39 children

How many like either Penelope Lively or Anne Fine?
12 children

How many children like either Penelope Lively or Dick King Smith?
18 children

How many more children like Roald Dahl than the other three together?
18 children

How many do not like Anne Fine?
57 children

80 children were asked what their hobbies were. The pie chart shows the results.

How many children like reading?
12 children

How many more children do sport than make models?
4 children

How many children either read or collect stamps for a hobby?
32 children

How many children do not like computer games?
64 children

On this page children have to find percentages of amounts. If they are unsure, remind them to divide the amount by 100, so producing a fraction, and then multiply by the required percentage.

Interpreting pie charts ☆

120 Year 6 children were surveyed to find out what type of home they lived in.

How many children lived in terraced houses?
20% of 120 is 24.
24 children

How many children lived in flats?
10% of 120 is 12.
12 children

A group of 40 children recorded their eye colours.

How many had blue eyes?
12

How many had either hazel or green eyes?
10

How many more had brown eyes than grey?
14

How many did not have hazel eyes?
34

As part of a school project, Lar records the colours of 150 cars in his local supermarket's car park. He records his information on a pie chart.

How many blue cars were there?
51

How many yellow cars were there?
12

How many people did not drive a red car?
111

How many people did not drive green or white cars?
102

Children are required to find percentages of amounts. If they are unsure, remind them to divide the amount by 100, producing a fraction, and then multiply by the required percentage. Make sure that they understand what the questions require.

Drawing 2D shapes

Congruent shapes are shapes that have angles and sides of exactly the same size.

These shapes are congruent because they can be fitted exactly on top of each other.

Measure the angles and sides of these shapes and draw a congruent shape next to each one.

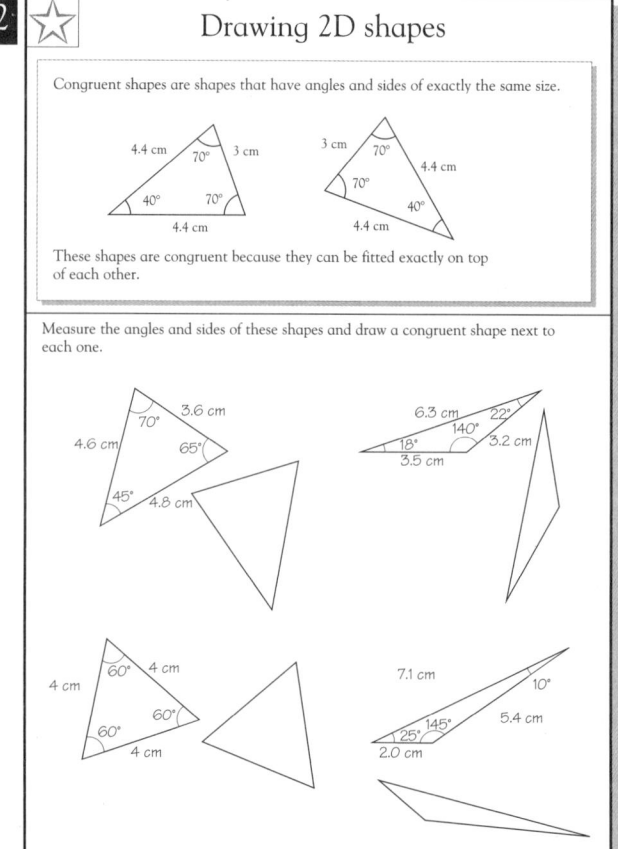

If children experience difficulty with triangles, check the measurements of the angles and sides. It is better to avoid drawing a mirror image of the shape as the relationship between angles and sides may cause confusion.